James Martineau

Modern Materialism in its Relations to Religion and Theology

James Martineau

Modern Materialism in its Relations to Religion and Theology

ISBN/EAN: 9783337252038

Printed in Europe, USA, Canada, Australia, Japan

Cover: Foto ©Suzi / pixelio.de

More available books at **www.hansebooks.com**

IN ITS RELATIONS TO

RELIGION AND THEOLOGY

Comprising an Address delivered in Manchester New College, October 6th, 1874, and Two Papers reprinted from "The Contemporary Review"

BY

JAMES MARTINEAU, LL.D

WITH AN INTRODUCTION BY

HENRY W. BELLOWS, D.D

NEW YORK
G. P. PUTNAM'S SONS
No. 182 Fifth Avenue
1877

PREFACE.

The following Address, published by desire of my College, was much curtailed in oral delivery. As somewhat more patience may be hoped for in a reader than in a hearer, it now appears in full. The position assumed in it, of resistance to some speculative tendencies of modern physical research, is far from congenial to me: for it seems to place me in the wrong camp. But the exclusive pretension, long set up by Theology, to dominate the whole field of knowledge, seems now to have simply passed over to the material Sciences;—with the effect of inverting, rather than removing, a mischievous intellectual confusion, and shifting the darkness from outward Nature to Morals and Religion. I cannot admit that these are conquered provinces: and to re-affirm their independence, and protest against their absorption in a universal material empire, appears to me a pressing need alike for true philosophy and for the future of human character and society.

LONDON, Oct. 12, 1874.

INTRODUCTION.

Is the mind of man only the last product of the matter and force of our system of Nature, having its origin in the blind or purposeless chance which drifts into order and intelligence under a self-executing mandate or necessity, called the survival of the fittest? The alleged discovery and partial verification of the *method* by which Nature works, has aroused suspicions in many leading scientific minds that Nature is the only and the final reality; that we cannot get behind her phenomena—or rather, that there is nothing behind them; that matter and force are all we know or need to know, and that they have answered so many of our questions in regard to the origin of animal existence and instincts, and even human intelligence, that they need only to be persistently pressed in the same direction to tell us all we can ever know and all we ought to believe.

It is certain that a spirit older than matter, an intelligence other than human, a will freer than necessity, does not enter into the causes of things contemplated by the new science. It studies a mindless universe with the sharpened instincts of brutes who have slowly graduated into men—themselves the most intelligent essences in existence. Consciousness, reason, purpose, will, are results of blind, undesigning, unfeeling forces, inherent in matter. God is an unknown and unknowable Being, if He exists; but He is a needless hypothesis, and really only the reflection of man's own God-like thoughts and feelings. In its childhood humanity invented Him as the hiding-place of its own ignorance! It is against this hypothesis that Mr. Martineau directs his battery in the discourse which follows.

It is refreshing, in the midst of the crude replies which alarmed religionists are hastily hurling at the scientific assailants of faith in a living God, to hear one thoroughly furnished scholar, profound metaphysician, and earnest Christian, entering his thoughtful and deeply-considered protest against the tendencies or conclusions of modern Materialism. Throughout the whole discussion of the last ten years, between utilitarian philosophers and scientific materialists, on one side, and believers in intuitive morals and spiritual realities on the other, Mr. Martineau has confessedly been the leading champion of faith. No writer has rendered, in this generation, such service to Religion, assailed in its vital assumptions by the arrogance of science, drunk with the new wine of its recent victories. Happily unhampered with theological anachronisms or ecclesiastical entanglements; free to acknowledge all that science and experience can justly allege against dogmatic inventions or out-lived traditions; a frank confessor of whatever new facts in the genesis of Nature modern science has established; tied to no creed and confessing no intellectual accountableness to any power less than the Eternal Reason—Mr.

Martineau, by his nature, culture, age, position, and character, is, of all living men, the best fitted to speak with the scientific mind of the day in the interests of religious faith, and more likely to be listened to by it with respect than any other voice. It is not as an enemy of science, much less as a friend of superstition; not as a disputer of the method of the Evolutionists, far less as a defender of bibliolatry or popular theology, that Mr. Martineau appears, but as one who hails and blesses all new truth derived from scientific sources, and especially in its influence in dispelling theological assumptions and time-hardened errors, himself a firm believer in spiritual realities and in a personal God.

It is instructive to find the disowned leaders in theological reform among the stoutest defenders of the essential postulates of religious faith, and to recognize in the foremost champions of spiritual realities against the assaults of modern Materialism, the knights who have swung the most ponderous battle-axes at the errors and exaggerations of what is called "orthodoxy." It must be a great puzzle to the English people to discover, in the stoutest, keenest, and most competent defender of essential Religion, openly assailed by the most gifted scientific minds, the person of a non-conformist Minister, representative of a body more neglected, disfellowshiped, and popularly associated with the enemies of faith, than any other in Christendom. It is a noble return to the church for the life-long suspicion and alienation it has visited upon one of its purest and most enlightened sons.

James Martineau needs no introduction to American thinkers, and I have not the presumption, in writing at the request of the American publishers this preface to his latest work, to hope to add anything to the attention this profound and brilliant paper will receive. I seek rather to avail myself of its attraction to win a little notice to suggestions that would find small audience out of such company.

RELIGION

AS AFFECTED BY

MODERN MATERIALISM.

The College which places me here to-day professes to select and qualify suitable men for the Nonconformist Ministry; that is, the headship of societies voluntarily formed for the promotion of the Christian life. In carrying out its work, two rules have been invariably observed: (1) the Special Studies which deal with our sources of religious faith—whether in the scrutiny of nature or in the interpretation of sacred books—have been left open to the play of all new lights of thought and knowledge, and have promptly reflected every well-grounded intellectual change; and (2) the General Studies which give the balanced aptitudes of a cultivated mind have been made as extensive and thorough as the years at disposal would allow. In both these rules there is apparent a genuine thirst for a right apprehension of things, a contempt for the dangers of possible discovery, a persuasion that in the mind most large and luminous the springs of Religion have the freshest and the fullest flow ; together with the idea that the Preacher, instead of being the organ of a given theology, should himself, by the natural influence of mental superiority, pass to the front and take the lead in a regulated growth of opinion.

There have never been wanting prophets of ill who distrusted this method as rash. So much open air does not suit the closet divine ; such liability to change disappoints the fixed idea of the partisan ; and the " practical man " does not want his preacher's head made heavy with too much learning, or his faith attenuated in the vacuum of metaphysics. At the present moment these partial distrusts are superseded by a deeper and more comprehensive misgiving, affecting not the method

simply, but the aim and function of our
Institution. Side by side with the literary
pursuits of the scholar, the study of external
nature has always had a place of honor in our
traditions and our estimates of a manly education;
and there is scarcely a special science
which has not some brilliant names that
range not far from the lines of our history;
and from the favorite shelf of all our libraries,
the Principia of Newton, the Essays of
Franklin, the Papers of Priestley and Dalton,
the " Principles " of Lyell, the Biological
Treatises of Southwood Smith and Carpenter,
and the records of Botanical research by Sir
James Smith and the Hookers, look down
upon us with something of a personal interest.
The successive enlargements given by these
skilled interpreters to our earlier picture of
the world—the widening Space, the deepening
vistas of Time, the new groups of chemical
elements and the precision of their combinations,
the detected marvels of physiological
structure, and the rapid filling-in of
missing links in the chain of organic life—

have been eagerly welcomed as adding a glory to the realities around, and, by the erection of fresh shrines and cloisters, turning the simple temple in which we once stood into a clustered magnificence. Thus it was, so long as discoveries came upon us one by one ; nor did any biblical chronology or Apocalypse interfere with their proper evidence for an hour. But *now*—must we not confess it?—certain shadows of anxiety seem to steal forth and mingle with the advancing light of natural knowledge, and temper it to a less genial warmth. It comes on, no longer in the simple form of pulse after pulse of positive and limited discovery, but with the ambitious sweep of a universal theory, in which facts given by observation, laws gathered by induction, and conceptions furnished by the mind itself, are all wrought up together as if of homogeneous validity. A report is thus framed of the Genesis of things, made up, indeed, of many true chapters of Science, but systematized by the terms and assumptions of a questionable, if not an untenable, philosophy. To the inexpert reader this report seems to be all of one piece; and he is disturbed to find an account apparently complete of the " Whence and the Whither" of all things without recourse to aught that is divine; to see the refinements of organism and exactitudes of adaptation disenchanted of their wonder; to watch the beauty of the flower fade into a necessity; to learn that Man was never *intended* for his place upon this scene, and has no commission to fulfill, but is simply flung hither by the competitive passions of the most gifted brutes; and to be assured that the élite beings that tenant the earth tread each upon an infinite series of failures, and survive as trophies of immeasurable misery and death. Thus an apprehension has become widely spread, that Natural History and Science are destined to give the *coup de grâce* to all theology, and discharge the religious phenomena from human life; that churches and their symbols must disappear like the witches' chamber and the astrologists' tower; and that, as everything above our nature is dark and void, those who affect to lift it lead it nowhither, and must take themselves away as "blind leaders of the blind." Whether this apprehension is well founded or not is a very grave question for society in many relations; and is emphatically urgent for those who educate men as spiritual guides to others, and who can invest them with no directing power except the native force of a mind at one with the truth of things and a heart of quickened sympathies. Hitherto, they have been trained under the assumptions that the Universe which includes us and folds us round is the Life-dwelling of an Eternal Mind; that the World of our abode is the scene of a Moral Government incipient but not yet complete; and that the upper zones of Human Affection, above the clouds of self and passion, take us into the sphere of a Divine Communion. Into this over-arching scene it is that growing thought and enthusiasm have expanded to catch their light and fire. And if "the new faith" is to carry in it the contradictories of

these positions—if it leaves us to make what we can of a simply molecular universe, and a pessimist world, and an unappeasable battle of life—it will require another sort of Apostolate, and would make such a difference in the studies which it is reasonable to pursue, that it might be wisest for us to disband, and let the new Future preach its own gospel, and devise, if it can, the means of making the tidings "*glad*." Better at once to own our occupation gone than to linger on sentimental sufferance, and accept the indulgent assurance that, though there is no longer any *truth* in religion, there is some nice feeling in it; and that while, for all we have to teach, we might shut up to-morrow, we may harmlessly keep open still, as a nursery of "*Emotion.*"*
I trust that, when "emotion" proves empty, we shall stamp it out, and get rid of it.

Though, however, no partnership between the physicist and the theologian can be formed on these terms of assigning the intellect to

---

* See Professor Tyndall's Address before the British Association; with Additions, p. 61.

the one and the feelings to the other, may it not be that, in the flurry of exultation and of panic, they misconstrue their real position? and that their relations, when calmly surveyed, may not be in such a state of tension as each is ready to believe? Looking on their respective contentions from the external position of logical observation, and without presuming to call in question the received inductions of the naturalist, I believe that both parties mistake the bearing of those inductions upon Religion; and that, although this bearing is in some aspects serious, it is neither of the quality nor of the magnitude frequently ascribed to it. I venture to affirm that the essence of Religion, summed up in the three assumptions already enumerated, is independent of any possible results of the natural sciences, and stands fast through the various readings of the Genesis of things.

The unpracticed mind of simple times goes out, it is true, upon everything *en masse*, and indeterminately feels and thinks about itself and the field of its existence, the inner and the outer, the transient and the permanent, the visible and the invisible: its knowledge and its worship, the pictures of its fancy and the intuition of its faith, are as yet a single tissue, of which every broken thread rends and deforms the whole. Hence the oldest sacred traditions run into stories of world-building; and the earliest attempts at a systematic interpretation of nature, in which physical ideas were clothed in mythical garb, are regarded by Aristotle as "*theological.*" It must be admitted that our own age has not yet emerged from this confusion. And in so far as Church belief is still committed to a given cosmogony and natural history of Man, it lies open to scientific refutation, and has already received from it many a wound under which it visibly pines away. It is needless to say that the *new* "book of Genesis," which resorts to Lucretius for its "first beginnings," to protoplasm for its fifth day, to "natural selection" for its Adam and Eve, and to evolution for all the rest, contradicts the *old* book at every point; and inasmuch as it dissipates the dream of Paradise, and removes the tragedy of the Fall, cancels at once the need and the scheme of Redemption, and so leaves the historical churches of Europe crumbling away from their very foundations. If any one would know how utterly unproducible in modern daylight is the theology of the symbolical books, how absolutely alien from the real springs of our life, let him follow for a few hours the newest movement of ecclesiastical reform, and listen to the reported conferences at Bonn on the remedies for a divided Christendom. Scarcely could the personal reappearance of Athanasius or Cyril on the floor of the council-hall be more startling, or the cries of anathema from the voices of the ancient dead have a more wondrous sound, than the reproduction, as hopes of the future, by men of Munich, of Chester, of Pittsburg, and of the Eastern Church, of formulas without meaning for the present, the eager discussion of subtle varieties of falsehood, and the anxious masking of their differences by opaque phrases under which everybody manages to look. Such signs of strange intellectual anachronism excuse the aversion with which many a thoughtful man, with a heart still full of reverence, turns away from all religious association, and lives without a church. It has been the infatuation of ecclesiastics to miss the inner divine spirit that breathes through the sources of their faith, and to seize, as the materials of their system, the perishable conceptions and unverified predictions of more fervent but darker times; so that, in the structure they have raised, all that is most questionable in the legacy of the past — obsolete Physics, mythical History, Messianic Mythology, Apocalyptic prognostications — have been built into the very walls, if not made the corner-stone, and now by their inevitable decay threaten the whole with ruin. Why, indeed, should I charge this infatuation on councils and divines alone? It is not professional, but human; it is a delusion which affects us all. We are forever shaping our representations of invisible things, in comparison with other men's notions, into forms of definite opinion, and throwing them to the front, as if they were the photographic equivalent of our real faith. Yet somehow the essence of our religion never finds its way into these frames of theory: as we put them together it slips away, and, if we turn to pursue it, still retreats behind; ever ready to work with the will, to unbind and sweeten the affections, and bathe the life with reverence; but refusing to be seen, or to pass from a divine hue of thinking into a human pattern of thought. The effects of this infatuation in the founders of our civilization are disastrous on both sides, not only to the Churches whose system is undermined, but to the spirit of the Science which undermines it. It turns out that, with the sun and moon and stars, and in and on the earth both before and after the appearance of our race, quite other things have happened than those which the consecrated cosmogony recites: especially Man, instead of falling from a higher state, has risen from a lower, and inherits, instead of a uniform corruption, a law of perpetual improvement; so that the real process has the effect, not only of an enormous magnifier, but of an inverting mirror, on the theological picture. Yet, notwithstanding the deplorable appearance to which that picture is thus reduced, it is exhibited afresh every week to millions still taught to regard it as divine. This is the mischief on the theologic side. On the other hand, Science, in executing this merited punishment, has borrowed from its opponents one of their worst errors, in identifying the anomalous or lawless with the divine, and assuming that whatever falls within the province of nature drops thereby out of relation to God. As the old story of Creation called in the Supreme Power only by way of supernatural paroxysm, to gain some fresh start beyond the resources of the natural order, so the new inquirers, on getting rid of these crises, fancy that the Agent who had been invoked for them is gone, and proclaim at once that Matter without Thought is competent to all. In thus confounding the idea of the Divine Mind with that of *miracle-worker*, they do but go over to the theological camp, and snatch thence its oldest and bluntest weapon, which in modern conflict can only burden the hand that wields it. How runs the history of their alleged negative discovery? The Naturalist was told in his youth that at certain intervals—at the joints, for instance, between successive species of organisms—acts of sudden creation summoned fresh groups of creatures out of nothing. These epochs he attacks with riper knowledge; he finds a series of intermediary forms, and fragmentary lines of suggestion for others; and when the affinities are fairly complete, and the chasm in the order of production is filled up, he turns upon us, and says, "See, there is no break in the chain of origination, however far back you trace it; we no more want a Divine Agent *there* and *then*, than *here* and *now*." Be it so; but it is precisely here and now that He is needed, to be the fountain of orderly power, and to render the tissue of laws intelligible by his presence: his witness is found not only in the gaps, but in the continuity of being—not in the suspense, but in the everlasting flow of change; for the universe as known, being throughout a system of *Thought-relations*, can subsist only in an eternal Mind that thinks it.

In the whole history of the Genesis of things Religion must unconditionally surrender to the Sciences. Not indeed that it is without share in the great question of *Causality;* but its concern with it is totally different from theirs; for it asks only about the "*Whence*" of all phenomena, while they concentrate their scrutiny upon the "*How:*" by which I mean that their end is accomplished as soon as it has been found in what groups phenomena regularly cluster, and on what threads of succession they are strung, and into what classification their resemblances throw them. These are matters of fact, directly or circuitously ascertainable by perception, and remaining the same, *be their originating power what it may*. On *that* ulterior question the Sciences have nothing to say. And, on the other hand, when Religion here takes up her word and insists that the phenomena thus reduced to system are the product of *Mind*, she in no way prejudges the *modus operandi*, but is ready to accept whatever affinities of aspect, whatever adjustments of order, the skill of observers may reveal. On *these* investigations she has nothing to say. If indeed you could ever show that the method of the universe is one along which *no Mind could move*—that it is absolutely incoherent and unideal—you would destroy the possibility of Religion as a doctrine of Causality: only, however, by simultaneously discovering the impossibility of Science—which wholly consists in organizing the phenomena of the world into an intellectual scheme reflecting the structure of its archetype. That those who labor to render the universe *intelligible* should call in question its *relation to intelligence*, is one of those curious inconsistencies to which the ablest specialists are often the most liable when meditating in foreign fields. If it takes *Mind* to construe the world, how can the negation of Mind suffice to constitute it?

It is not in the history of Superstition alone that the human mind may be found struggling in the grasp of some mere nightmare of its own creation : a philosophical hypothesis may sit upon the breast with a weight not less oppressive and not more real; till a friendly touch or a dawning light breaks the spell, and reveals the quiet morning and the bed of rest. Is there, for instance, no logical illusion in the Materialist doctrine which in our time is proclaimed with so much pomp and resisted with so much passion? "Matter is all I want," says the Physicist : " give me its atoms alone, and I will explain the universe." "Good; take as many of them as you please : see, they have all that is requisite to Body, being homogeneous extended solids." "That is not enough," he replies; "it might do for Democritus and the mathematicians, but I must have somewhat more : the atoms must be not only in motion and of various shapes, but also of as many kinds as there may be chemical elements; for how could I ever get water, if I had only hydrogen molecules to work with?" "So be it," we shall say; "only this is a considerable enlargement of your specified datum,

—in fact, a conversion of it into several; yet, even at the cost of its monism, your scheme seems hardly to gain its end; for by what manipulation of your resources will you, for example, educe *consciousness?* No organism can ever show you more than Matter moved; and, as Dubois-Reymond observes, there is an impassable chasm 'between definite movements of definite cerebral atoms and the primary facts which I can neither define nor deny—*I feel pain or pleasure, I taste a sweetness, smell a rose-scent, hear an organ tone, see red,* together with the no less immediate assurance they give, *therefore I exist:*' 'it remains,' he adds, 'entirely and forever inconceivable that it should signify a jot to a number of carbon and hydrogen and nitrogen and oxygen and other atoms how they lie and move;' 'in no way can one see how from their concurrence consciousness can arise.'*

---

* "Ueber die Grenzen des Naturerkennens," p. 29. Compare p. 20. "I will now prove, as I believe in a very cogent way, not only that, in the present state of our knowledge, Consciousness cannot be explained by

What say you to this problem?" "It does not daunt me at all," he declares: "of course you understand that my atoms have all along been affected by gravitation and polarity; and now I have only to insist, with Fechner,* on a difference among molecules; there are the *inorganic*, which can change only their *place*, like the particles in an undulation; and there are the *organic*, which can change their *order*, as in a globule that turns itself inside out. With an adequate number of these, our problem will be manageable." "Likely enough," we may say, "seeing how careful you are to provide for all emergencies; and if any hitch should occur at the next step, where you will have to pass from mere sentiency to Thought and Will, you can again look in upon your atoms, and fling among them a handful of Leibnitz's monads, to serve as souls in little,

---

its material conditions,—which perhaps every one allows,—but that from the very nature of things it never will admit of explanation by these conditions."

* Einige Ideen zur Schöpfungs- und Entwickelungsgeschichte der Organismen, §§ i. ii.

and be ready, in a latent form, with that *Vorstellungsfähigkeit* which our picturesque interpreters of nature so much prize. But surely you must observe how this 'Matter' of yours alters its style with every change of service: starting as a beggar, with scarce a rag of 'property' to cover its bones, it turns up as a Prince, when large undertakings are wanted, loaded with investments, and within an inch of a plenipotentiary. In short, you give it precisely what you require to take from it; and when your definition has made it 'pregnant with all the future,' there is no wonder if from it all the future might be born."

"We must radically change our notions of Matter," says Professor Tyndall; and then, he ventures to believe, it will answer all demands, carrying "the promise and potency of all terrestrial life."* If the measure of the required "change in our notions" had been

---

* Address before the British Association; with Additions, pp. 54, 55. Compare the statement, by Dubois-Reymond, of the opposite opinion, quoted supra, p. 28, note.

specified, the proposition would have had a real meaning, and been susceptible of a test. Without this precision, it only tells us, "Charge the word potentially with your quæsita, and I will promise to elicit them explicitly." It is easy traveling through the stages of such an hypothesis; you deposit at your bank a round sum ere you start; and, drawing on it piecemeal at every pause, complete your grand tour without a debt. Words, however, ere they can hold such richness of prerogative, will be found to have emerged from their physical meaning, and to be truly $\Theta εοφόρα\ ὀνόματα$, —terms that bear God in them, and thus dissolve the very theory which they represent. Such extremely clever Matter—Matter that is up to everything, even to writing Hamlet, and finding out its own evolution, and substituting a molecular plébiscite for a divine monarchy of the world, may fairly be regarded as a little too modest in its disclaimer of the attributes of Mind.

Nor is the fallacy escaped by splitting our datum into two, and instead of crowding all requisites into Matter, leaving it on its old slender footing, and assuming along with it *Force* as a distinct entity. The two postulates will perform their promise, just like the one, on condition that you secrete within them in the germ all that you are to develop from them as their fruit; and in this case the word "*Force*" is the magical seed-vessel which is to surprise us with the affluence of its contents. The surprise is due to one or two nimble-witted substitutions, of which a conjuror might be proud, whereby unequals are shown to be equals, and out of an acorn you hatch a chicken. First, the noun *Force* is sent into the plural (which of course is only itself in another form), and so we get provided with several of them. Next, as there is now a class, the members must be distinguishable; and, as they are all of them activities, they will be known one from another by the sort of work they do: one will be a mechanician—another a chemist—a third will be a swift runner along the tracks of life—a fourth will find out all the rest—will do our reasoning about them, and get up all our examinations for us. The last of these, every one must own —at least every one who has been graduated— is much more dignified than the others; and all through we rise, at every step, from ruder to more refined accomplishment. With things thus settled, we seem to have found Plato's ideal State, in which every order minds its own business, and no element presumes to cross the line and become something else. Not so, however; for, after thus differencing the forces and keeping them under separate covers, the next step is to unify them, and show them all as the homogeneous contents of a single receptacle. The forces, we are assured, are interchangeable, and relieve each other; when one has carried its message, it hands the torch to another, and the light is never quenched or the race arrested, but runs an eternal round. But why then, you will say, divide them first, only to unite them afterwards? Follow our logical wonder-worker one move further, and you will see. He has now, we may say, his four vessels standing on the table; the contents of the whole are to be whisked into one; having them all, he has more ways than one of working out their equivalence; and it remains at his option, *which* he shall lift to let the mouse run out. For some reason, best known to himself, he never thinks of choosing the last; indeed it is pretty much to avoid this, and obtain other receptacles *empty of thought*, that he broke down the original unity. If he be a circumspect physiologist, he will probably prefer the third, and exhibit the universal principle as in some sense *living;* if he be a daring physicist, he will lay hold of the first, and pronounce *mechanical* dynamics good enough for the cosmos.

Am I asked to indicate the precise seat of fallacy in the hypothesis which I have ventured to criticise? The alleged division of forces, considered as something over and above the phenomena ascribed to them, is absolutely without ground; each of them, as apart from any other, has a purely ideal existence, without the slightest claim to objective reality.

Science, dividing its labors, has to break down phenomena into sets, according to their resemblances and the affinities of their conditions; it disposes them thus into natural provinces, the laws of which, when ascertained, give us the rules by which the phenomena assort themselves or successively arise—but nothing more. But whatever field we survey, we carry into it the belief, inherent in the constitution of the intellect itself, of a Causal Power as the source of every change: we believe it for each, we believe it for all: it repeats itself identically with every instance; and when a multitude of instances are tied up together in virtue of their similarity and made into a class, this constantly recurring reference, this identity of relation to a power behind, is marked by giving that power a singular name; as the phenomena of weight are labeled with the title *Gravitation*, expressing unity in their causal relation. Were we closeted with this group of facts alone, this unity would live in our minds without a rival, and we should have no numerical distinction in our account of force.

But, meanwhile, other observers have been going through a like experience in some separate field; have gleaned and bound into a sheaf its scattered mass of homogeneous growths, and denoted them by another name —say, *Electricity*—carrying in it the same haunting reference to a source for them all. Now, why is this a *new* name? Is it that we have found a new *power*? Have we carried our observation *behind the phenomena*, so as, in either instance, to find any power at all? Are the two cases differenced by anything else than the dissimilarity of their phenomena? Run over these distinctions, and, when you have exhausted them, is there anything left by which you can compare and set apart from each other the respective producing forces? All these questions must be answered in the negative; the differentiations lie only in the effects; the causal power is not *observed*, but *thought;* and that thought is the same, not only from instance to instance, but from field to field; and by this sameness it cancels plurality from Force, and reduces the story of their transmigration into a scientific mythology. The distinctive names, therefore, mark only differences in the *sets of phenomena;* they are simply instruments of classification for noticeable changes in nature, and carry no partitions into the mysterious depths behind the scenes. The dynamic catalogue being thus left empty and cut down to a single term, do we talk nonsense when we attach qualifying epithets to the word *Force,* and speak of "*electric force,*" of "*nerve force,*" of "*polar force,*" etc.? Not so; provided we mean by those phrases simply, *Force, quantum sufficit,* now for *one set of phenomena, now for another,* without implication of other difference than that of the seat and conditions and aspect of the manifestations. But the moment we step across this restriction, we are in the land of myths.

Power, then, is one and undivided. As external causality, it is not an *object of knowledge,* but an *element given in the relations of knowledge, a condition of our thinking of phenomena at all.* Were this all, our necessary belief in it would be unattended by any *representation* of it; it would remain an intellectual notion (Begriff), and we could no more bring it before the mind under any definite type than we can the meaning of such words as "substance" and "possibility." In one field, however, and no more, it falls into coincidence with our experience; for we ourselves put forth power in the exercise of Will and are personally conscious of Causality; and this sample of *immediate* knowledge because *self*-knowledge supplies us with the means of *representing* to ourselves what else we should have to *think* without a type. Here, accordingly, we reach, I venture to affirm, what we really mean, and what alone saves us from the mere empty form of meaning, whenever we assent to the axiom of Causality. It is very true that the exercise of Will, having more or less of complication, itself admits of analysis; *intention* may play a larger or smaller part, may leave less or more for the share of automatic or impulsive activity; and by letting the former withdraw into the background of our conception, we may come to think of *causation apart from purpose*—which,

I suppose, is the *idea of Force*. But this is a bare fiction of abstraction, shamming an integral reality; an old soldier pensioned off from actual duty, but allowed to wear his uniform and look like what he was. Since we have to assume causality for all things, and the only causality we know is that of living mind, that type has no legitimate competitor. Even if it had, its sole adequacy would leave it in possession of the field. For among the products to be accounted for is the whole class and hierarchy of *minds;* and unless there is to be more in the effect than in the cause, nothing less than Mind is competent to realize a scheme of being whose ranks ascend so high. As for the plea—which has unhappily passed into a common-place—that, even if it be so, that transcendent object is beyond all cognizance—I will only say that this doctrine of Nescience stands in exactly the same relation to causal power, whether you construe it as Material Force or as Divine Agency. Neither can be *observed;* one or the other must be *assumed.* If you admit to the category of knowledge only what we learn by observation, particular or generalized, then is Force unknown; if you extend the word to what is imported by the intellect itself into our cognitive acts, to make them such, then is God known.

This comment on current hypotheses refers to them only so far as they overstep the limits of Science, and aspire to the seat of judgment on ulterior questions of philosophy. So long as they simply descend upon this or that realm of nature, and try their strength there in simplifying its laws or rendering them deducible —or, passing from province to province, labor to formulate equations available for several or for all—they must be respectfully left to pursue their work; and whenever their authors present their demonstrated "system of the world," all reasonable men will learn it from them, whatever it may be, as scholars from a master. In the investigation of the genetic order of things, Theology is an intruder, and must stand aside. Religion first reaches its true ground, when, leaving the problem of what *has happened*, it takes its stand on what *forever is.** I do not say that it is indifferent to us how antecedent ages have been filled, and have brought up the march with which we fall into step to-day; for we are beings of large perspective, concentrating in us many lines of distance and images that lie between

---

* This statement has been pronounced by a friendly critic (*Spectator*, Oct. 17, p. 1293) "not only questionable, but gravely misleading;" as implying "that if history and science showed us constant degradation instead of evolution of higher forms, and filled us with anticipations from which reasonable hope—hope, that is, measured by experience—was utterly excluded, the religion of the Soul would just as certainly assert the supremacy of righteousness and the love of God, as she does with the united voices of revelation and experience to help her out."

If I had said that Religion has *no interest* in the history of nature and the world, this criticism would have been just. But I cannot see how it applies to the positions which the text aims to make good, viz.: that Religion has no *locus standi* in investigations about the order of phenomena in the past, but must make what it can of that order as determined by scientific evidence: and that Religion has a *locus standi*, where Science has not, in the quest and cognition of the Cause that is behind all phenomena. To reach that Cause, there is no need to go into the past, as though, being missed here, He could be found there. But when once He has been discerned through the proper organs of divine apprehension, the whole life of humanity is recognized as the

the eye and the horizon ; and what we see at
hand borrows a portion of its aspect from relation to remoter zones behind. But still, if
the light were all turned off from the Past,
and on facing it we looked only into the Night,
the reality for us is not *there*, but *here*, where
it is Day. However the present may have
come about, I find myself in it : in whatever
way my faculties may have been determined,
faculties they are, and they give me insight
into my duty and outlook on my position :
however the world, of Nature and of Society,
may have grown to what it is, its scene contains me, its relations twine around me, its
physiognomy appeals to me with a meaning
from behind itself. If these data do not
suffice to show me my kinship with what is
above, below, around me, and find my moral
and spiritual place, I shall not be greatly

---

scene of His agency, and the past, no less than the present, has to be embraced in the religious interpretation of
the world, and becomes an object of sacred interest.
Though Religion, in taking its stand on what forever
is, *first reaches* its true ground, it does not follow that it
must always remain there.

helped by discovering how many ages my constitution has been upon the stocks, and its antecedents been upon the way. The beings that touch me with their look and draw me out of myself, the duties that press upon my heart and hand, are on the spot, speaking to me while the clock ticks; and to love them aright, to serve them faithfully, and construct with them a true harmony of life, is the same task, whether I bear within me the inheritance of a million years, or, with all my surroundings, issued this morning from the dark.

Remaining then at home, and consulting the nature which we have and which we see, we find that, far from being self-inclosed, or related only to its visible dependencies, it turns a face, on more than one side, right towards the Infinite, and, often to the disregard of nearer things, moves hither or thither as if shrinking from a shadow advancing thence, or drawn by a light that wins it forward. We are constantly—even the most practical of us—seeing what is invisible and hearing what is inaudible, and permitting them to send us on our way. Not left, like the mere animal, to be the passive resultant of forces without and instincts within, but invested with an alternative power, we are conscious partners in the architecture of our own character, and know ourselves to be the bearers of a *trust;* and this fiduciary life takes us at once across the boundary which separates nature from what transcends it. Seducing appetites and turbulent passions and ignoble ease never gain our undivided ear; while we bend to them, there are pleading voices which distract us, and which, if they do not save us, follow us with an expostulating shame. Nor, if ever we wake up and kindle at the appeal of misery and the cry of wrong, or with the spontaneous fire of disinterested affection or devotion to the true and good, can we construe them into anything less than a Divine claim upon us: we know their right over us at a glance; we feel on us their look of authority in reply; if, to our careless fancy, we were ever our own, we can be so no more. Once stirred by the higher springs of character, and possessed by the yearning for the perfect mind, we are aware that to live out of these is our supreme obligation, and that for us nothing short of this is holy. To have *seen* the vision of the best and possible and *not* to pursue it, is to mar the true idea of our nature, and to fall from its heaven as a rebel and an outcast. This inner life of Conscience and ideal aspiration supplies the elements and sphere of Religion; and the discovery of Duty is as distinctly relative to an Objective Righteousness as the perception of Form to an external Space: it is a bondage, with superficial reluctance, but with deeper consent, to an invisible Highest; and both moral Fear and moral Love stand before the face of an authority which is the eternal reality of the holy, just, and true. On the first view, you might expect that the stronger the enthusiasm for goodness, and the surer the recoil from ill, so much the fitter would the mind be to stand alone in its self-adequacy; yet it is precisely at such elevation that it most trusts in a Supreme Perfection to which it only faintly responds, and leans for support on that everlasting stay. The life of aspiration, attempting to nurse itself, soon pines and dies; it must breathe a diviner air, and take its thirst to unwasting springs; and wherever it settles into a quiet tension of the will, and an upturned look of the affections, it is sustained by habitual access to the Fountain of sanctity, and by the consciousness of an Infinite sympathy. Are not both the need and the existence of this objective sustaining power acknowledged by Mr. Matthew Arnold himself, when he insists on that strange entity, "That, not ourselves, *which makes for righteousness*"? By an abstraction, however, such a function cannot be discharged; nothing ever "makes for righteousness" but One who *is* righteous. To support and raise the less, there must be a greater; and that which does not think and will and love, whatever the drift of its blind power, may indeed be larger, but is not greater, than the sinning soul that longs for purity.

Now, so long as the devotee of Goodness is

possessed by a faith, not only in his own aspirations, but in an Infinite Mind which fosters and secures them as counterparts of the highest reality, it is of little moment ethically what theory he adopts of their mode of origin within him. Whether he takes them as intuitive data of his understanding, or, with Hartley, as a transfiguration of sensible interests into a disinterested glory, or, with Darwin and Spencer, as the latest refinement of animal instinct and discipline after percolating through uncounted generations,—that which he has reached—be it first or last—is at all events *the truth of things*, the primordial and everlasting certainty, in comparison with which all prior stages of training, if such there were, give but dim gropings and transient illusions. In Hartley himself, accordingly, a doctrine essentially materialistic and carrying in it the whole principle of Evolution, so far as it could be epitomized in the individual's life, easily blended with moral fervor and even a mystic piety; and, in Priestley, with a noble heroism of veracity and an unswerving confidence in the perfect government of the universe. But what if the process of atomic development be taken as the *Substitute for God*, not as His *method*? if you withdraw from the beginning all *Idea* of what is to come out at the end—all Model or Archetype to control and direct the procedure, and restrain the *possible* from running off indefinitely into the false and wrong? Do you suppose that the ethical results can be still the same? The inevitable difference, I think, few considerate persons will deny; and without attempt to measure its amount, its chief feature may be readily defined.

It was often said by both James and John Stuart Mill, that you do not alter, much less destroy, a feeling or sentiment by giving its history: from whatever unexpected sources its constituents may be gathered, when once their confluence is complete the current they form runs on the same, whether you know them or not. How true this may be is exemplified by the younger Mill himself; who, while resolving the moral sentiments into simple pleasure and pain, and moral obligation into a balance of happiness, yet nobly protested that he would rather plunge into eternal anguish than falsely bend before an unrighteous power. If so it be, then one in whom benevolence, honor, purity, had reached their greatest refinement and most decisive clearness would suffer no change of moral consciousness, on becoming convinced that it is a "poetic thrill" of his "ganglia"* induced by the long breaking-in through which his progenitors have passed, in conformity with the system of organic modification that has deprived him of his fur and his tail. In spite of the apparent incongruity, let us grant that his higher affections will speak to him exactly as before, and make their claims felt by the same tones of sacred authority, so that they continue to subdue him in reverence or lift him as with inspiration. The surrender to them of heart and will under these conditions, the vow to abide by them and live in them,

---

* Professor Tyndall's Address, p. 49.

may still deserve acknowledgment as *Religion* but, inasmuch as they have shrunk into mere unaccredited subjective susceptibilities, they have lost all support from Omniscient approval, and all presumable accordance with the reality of things. For what *are* these moral intensities of his nature, seen under his new lights? Whence is their message? With what right do they deliver it to him in that imperative voice? and, if it be slighted, prostrate him with unspeakable compunction? Are they an influx of Righteousness and Love from the life of the universe? Do they report the insight of beings more august and pure? No; they are capitalized "experiences of utility" and social coercion, the record of ancestral fears and satisfaction stored in his brain, and reappearing with divine pretensions, only because their animal origin is forgotten; or, under another aspect, they are the newest advantage won by gregarious creatures in "the struggle for existence." From such an origin it is impossible to extract credentials for any elevated claim; so that although low beginnings may lead, in the natural order, to what is better than themselves—as a Julia may be the mother of an Agrippina—yet in such case the superiority lies in new endowment, which is *not* contained in the inheritance. For such new endowment as we gain in the ascent from interest to conscience the theory of transmission cannot provide. If the coarse and turbid springs of barbarous life, filtered through innumerable organisms, flow limpid and sparkling at last, the element is still the same, though the sediment is left behind; and as it would need a diviner power to turn the water into wine, so Prudence, run however fine, social Conformity, however swift and spontaneous, can never convert themselves into Obligation. Hence arises, I think, an inevitable contradiction between the scientific hypothesis and the personal characteristics of a high-souled disciple of the modern negative doctrine. For his supreme affections no adequate object and no corresponding source is offered in the universe; if they look back for their cradle, they see through the forest the cabin of the savage or the lair of the brute; if they look forth for their justifying reality and end, they fling vain arms aloft and embrace a vacancy. They cannot defend, yet cannot relinquish, their own enthusiasm: they bear him forward upon heroic lines that sweep wide of his own theory; and, transcending their own reputed origin and environment, they float upon vapors and are empty, self-poised by their own heat. One or two instances will illustrate the way in which what is best in our humanity is left, in the current doctrine, unsupported by the real constitution of the world.

Compassion—the instinctive response to the spectacle of misery—has a twofold expressiveness: it is in us a protesting vote against the sufferings we see, and a sign of faith that they are not ultimate, but remediable. Its singularity is, to be not one of these alone, but both. Were it a simple repugnance, it would drive us from its object; but it is an *aversion which attracts:* it snatches us with a bound to the very thing we hate, and not with hostile rush, but with softened tread and gentle words and uplifting hand. And what is the secret of this transfiguration of horror into love? It could never be but for the implicit assurance that for these wounds there is healing possible, if the nursing care does not delay. Should we not say then, if we trusted its own word about itself, that this principle, so deep and intense in our unfolded nature, is an evident provision for a world of *hopeful sorrow?* It is distinctly relative to pain, and would be out of place in a scene laid out for happiness alone; yet treats that pain as transient, and on passing into the cloud already sees the opening through. It enters the infirmary of human ills with the tender and cheerful trust of the young Sister of mercy, who binds herself to the perpetual presence of human maladies, that she may be forever giving them their discharge. Compassion institutes a strange order of servitude: it sets the strong to obey the weak, the man and woman to wait upon the child, and youth and beauty to kneel and bend before decrepitude and deformity. How then do the drift and faith of this instinct agree with the method of the outer world as now interpreted? Do they copy it exactly, and find encouragement from the great example? On the contrary, Nature, it is customary to say, is *pitiless*, and, while ever moving on, makes no step but by crushing a thousand-fold more sentient life than she ultimately sets up, and sets up none that does not devour what is already there. The battle of existence rages through all time and in every field; and its rule is to give no quarter—to dispatch the maimed, to overtake the halt, to trip up the blind, and drive the fugitive host over the precipice into the sea. Nature is fond of the mighty, and kicks the feeble; and, while forever multiplying wretchedness, has no patience with it when it looks up and moans. And so all-pervading is this rule, that evil, we are told, cannot really be put down, but only masked and diverted; if you suppress it here, it will break out there; the fire of anguish still rolls below and has alternate vents; when you stop up Ætna, it will blot out Sodom and Gomorrah, and bury the cities of the plain. Who can deny that such teachings as these set the outer universe and our inner nature at its best at hopeless variance with one another? Do they not depress the moral power to which we owe the most humanizing features of our civilization? We have not to go far for a practical answer. Within a few weeks the question has been raised whether the recent flow of commiseration towards the famine-stricken districts of India does not offend against the Law of Nature for reducing a superfluous population; and whether there were not advantages in the old method of taking no notice of these things, and letting Death pass freely over his threshing-floor and bury the human chaff quietly out of the way. Moral enthusiasm makes many a mischievous mistake in its haste and blindness, and greatly needs the guidance of wiser thought; but this tone of moral skepticism, which disparages the very springs of generous labor, and treats them as follies laughed at by the cynicism of Nature, is a thousand-fold more desolating. For it carries poison to the very roots of good. It is as the bursting-out of salt-springs in the valley of fruits; it soaks through the prolific soil of all the virtues, and turns the promise of Eden into a Dead Sea shore.

Beyond the range of the merely compassionate impulse, *Self-forgetfulness* in love for others has a foremost place in our ideal of character, and our deep homage as representing the true end of our humanity. We exact it from ourselves, and the poor answer we make to the demand costs us many a sigh; and till we can break the bonds that hold us to our own center, and lose our self-care in constant sacrifice, a shadow of silent reproach lies upon our heart. Who is so faultless, or so obtuse, as to be ignorant what shame there is, not only in snatched advantages and ease retained to others' loss, but in ungentle words, in wronging judgment within our private thoughts alone; nay, in simple blindness to what is passing in another's mind? Who does not upbraid himself for his slowness in those sympathies which are as a multiplying mirror to the joys of life, reflecting them in endless play? And the grace so imperfect in ourselves wins our instant veneration when realized in others. The historical admirations of men are often, indeed, drawn to a very different type of character: for Genius and Will have their magnificence as well as Goodness its beauty: but before the eye of a purified reverence, neither the giants of force nor the recluses of saintly austerity stand on so high a pedestal as the devoted benefactors of mankind. The heroes of honor are great; but the heroes of service are greater; nor does any appeal speak more home to us than a true story of life risked, of ambitions dropped, of repose surrendered, of temper molded, of all things serenely endured—perhaps unnoticed and in exile—at some call of sweet or high affection. Is then this religion of Self-sacrifice the counterpart of the behavior of the objective world? Is the same principle to be found dominating on that great scale? Far from it. *There*, we are informed, the only rule is *self-assertion:*

the all-determining Law is relentless competition for superior advantage; the condition of obeying which is, that you are to forego nothing, and never to miss an opportunity of pushing a rival over, and seizing the prey before he is on his feet again. We look without, and see the irresistible fact of selfish scramble: we look within, and find the irresistible faith of unselfish abnegation. So here, again, Morals are unnatural, and Nature is unmoral: and if, beyond Nature, there is nothing supreme in both relations to determine the subordination and resolve the contradiction, he who would be loyal to the higher call must be so without ground of trust; if he will not betray his secret ideal, he must follow it unverified, as a mystic enchantment of his own mind.

Once more: the *Sense of Duty* enforces the suggestions of these and other affections by an authority which we recognize as at once within us and over us, and making them more than *impulses*, more than *ideals*, and establishing them in *binding* relations with our Will.

The rudest self-knowledge must own that the consciousness of *Moral Obligation* is an experience *sui generis*, separated by deep distinctions from *outward necessity* on the one hand, and *inward desire* upon the other; and the only psychology which can bridge over these distinctions is that which escapes with its analysis into prehistoric ages, and finds it easy to grow vision out of touch, and read back all differentiation into sameness. No one would carry off the problem into that darkness who could deal with it in the present daylight: so, we may take it as confessed, that *to us* the suasion of Right speaks with a voice which no charming of pleasure and no chorus of opinion can ever learn to mimic. To disregard *them* is a simple matter of courage; we defy them, and are free: but if from *it* we turn away, we hear pursuing feet behind: and should we stop our ears, we feel upon us the grasp of an awful hand. Moral good would, in our apprehension, cease to be what it is, were it constituted by any natural good, or related to it otherwise than as its superior. It is not a *personal* end—one among the many satisfactions assigned to the separate activities of our constitution: else, it would be at our disposal, and we might forego it. Others are our partners in it: for it sets up *Rights* as counterparts to *Duties*, and widens by its reciprocity into a common element of Humanity. Is *that* then its native home? Have men created it, as an expression of their general wish—a concentrated code of civic police? We cannot rest in this: for no aggregate of wills, no public meeting of mankind, though it got together all generations and all contemporary tribes, could by vote make perfidy a virtue and turn pity into a crime. Moral Right is thus no *local* essence; but by its centrifugal force, relatively to our abode, slips off the earth and assumes an absolute universality as the law of all free agency. That it should present itself to us in this transcendent aspect is intelligible enough, if it be identified with the Universal Mind, and thence imparted to dependent natures permitted to be like Him: for, in that case, the related feelings and convictions are *true ;* in the order of reality, Righteousness *is* prior to the pains and pleasures of our particular faculties and the natural exigencies of our collective life ; and our allegiance is due to an eternal Perfection which penetrates the moral structure of all worlds. How, then, does this intuitive faith of our responsible will, this worship of an eternally Holy, stand with the cosmical conceptions now tyrannizing over the imaginations of men? It encounters the shock of contemptuous contradiction. Ethically, we are assured, the known world culminates in us. Before us, there was nothing morally good : over us, there is nothing morally better : Man himself is here the supreme being in the universe. In the just, the beneficent, the true, there is no pre-existence : they are not the roots of reality, but the last blossoms of the human phenomena. And even there, the fair show which gives them their repute of an ethereal beauty is but the play of an ideal light upon coarse materials ;— rude pleasures and ruder constraints are all that remain when the increments of fancy have fallen away. The real world provides *interests* alone ; which, when adequately masked, call themselves virtues and pass for something new : and, duped by this illusion, we dream of a realm of authoritative Duty, in which the earth is but a province of a supramundane moral empire. And so, we must conclude, the conscience which lives on this sublime but empty vision has transcended the tuition of Nature, and, in growing wiser than its teacher, has lost its foothold on reality, only to lean on a phantom of Divine support.

On the hypothesis of a Mindless universe, such is the fatal breach between the highest inward life of man and his picture of the outer world. All that is subjectively noblest turns out to be the objectively hollowest ; and the ideal, whether in life and character, or in the beauty of the earth and heaven, which he had taken to be the secret meaning of the Real, is repudiated by it, and floats through space as a homeless outcast. Even in this its desolation a devoted disciple will say, "I will follow thee whithersoever thou goest;" but how heavy the cross which he will have to bear! Religion, under such conditions, is a defiance of inexorable material laws in favor of a better which they have created but cannot sustain—a reaction of man against Nature, which he has transcended—a withdrawal of the Self which a resistless force pushes to the front—a preservation of the weak whom Necessity crushes, a sympathy with sufferings which life relentlessly sets up—a recognition of authoritative Duty which cannot be. Or will you perhaps insist that, in this contrariety between thought and fact, Religion must take the other side, discharge the $\vartheta\varepsilon\tilde{\iota}\alpha$ $o\nu\varepsilon\acute{\iota}\rho\alpha\tau\alpha$ as illusory, and in her homage hold fast to the solid world? This might perhaps in some sense be, if you only gave us a world which it was possible to respect. But, by a curious though intelligible affinity, the modern doctrine allies itself with an unflinching pessimism; it plays the cynic to the universe— penetrates behind its grand and gracious airs, and detects its manifold blunders and impostures: what skill it has it cannot help; and the only faults and horrors that are *not* in it are those which are too bad to live. Human life, which is the summit that has been won, is pronounced but a poor affair at best; and the scene which spreads below and around is but as a battle-field at night-fall, with a few victors taking their faint shout away, and leaving the plain crowded with wounds and vocal with agony. Existence itself, insists Hartmann, is an evil, in proportion as its range is larger and you know it more, and that of cultivated men is worst of all;* and the constitution of the world (so stupidly does it work) would be an unpardonable crime, did it issue from a power that knew what it was about.† How can these malcontents find any *Religion* in obeying such a power? Can they approach it with contumely at one moment, and with devotion at the next? If they think so ill of Nature, there can be no *reverence* in their ser-

---

* Philosophie des Unbewussten, c. xii., p. 598.
† Ap. Strauss: der alte und der neue Glaube, p. 223.

vice of her laws : on the contrary, they abandon what they revere, to bend before what they revile. To this humiliation the more magnanimous spirits will never stoop; they will find some excuse for still clinging to the ideal forms they cannot verify; will go apart with them with a high-toned love which stops short of faith, but is full of faithfulness; will linger near the springs of poetry and art, and there forget awhile the disenchanted Actual; and will wonder, perhaps, whether this half-consecrated ground may not suffice, when the temples are gone, to give an asylum to the worshipers. Such loyalty of heart towards the harmonies that *ought* to prevail, with disaffection towards the discords that *do* prevail, may indeed lift the character of a man to an elevation half divine; and in his presence, Nature, were she not blind, might start to see that she had produced a god. But, for all that, she is not going to succumb to him; she can call up her lower brood to suppress him, or monsters to chain him to her rock. He contends with the lower forces, believing them to be the stronger, and fights his losing battle against hordes of inferiors ever swarming to overwhelm what is too good for the world. Such religion as remains to him is a religion of despair—a pathetic defiance of an eternal baser power. And if there be anything tragic in earth or heaven, it is the proud desolation of a mind which has to regard itself as highest, to know itself the seat of some love and justice and devotion to the good, and to look upon the system of the universe as cruel, ugly, stupid, and mean. The most touching episodes of history are perhaps those which disclose the life of genius and virtue under some capricious and ignoble tyranny—asserting itself in the ostracism of an Aristides, the hemlock-cup of Socrates, the blood-bath of Thrasea; and no other than this is the life of every man who, walking only by his purest inner lights, finds that they illumine no nature but his own, and are baffled and quenched by the outer darkness.

It cannot be denied that there does exist this contrariety between the modern materialistic philosophy and religious faith. It cannot be believed that this contrariety is chargeable on any mutual contradiction among the human faculties themselves. Were we really placed between two informants that said "*Yes*" at the right ear, and "*No*" at the left, we should simply be without cognitive endowment at all, and all the pulsations of thought would cancel each other and die. Can we end the strife by separating the provinces of the two opposites, and saying that the function of the one is *to know*, of the other *to create?* * Certainly "creative" power is something grand, and Theology should perhaps feel honored to be invested with it. But, alas! a *known* materialism and a *created* God presents a combination which thought repudiates and reverence abhors; and the suggestion of which must be met with the counter-affirmations, that the atomic hypothesis is a thing *not known, but created;* while God is *not created, but*

---

* Professor Tyndall's Address, p. 64.

known. The only possible basis for a treaty of alliance between the tendencies now in conflict is not in lodging the one in the Reason, and the other in the Imagination, in order to keep them from quarreling, but in recognizing a duality in the functions of Reason itself, according as it deals with phenomena or their ground, with law or with causality, with material consecution or with moral alternatives, with the definite relations of space and time and motion, or with the indefinite intensities of beauty and values of affection which bear us to the infinitely Good. When once this adjustment of functions has been considerately made, the disturbed equilibrium of minds will be reinstated, the panic and the arrogance of our time will disappear, and the progress of the intellect will no longer shake the soul from her everlasting rest.

MODERN MATERIALISM:
ITS ATTITUDE TOWARDS THEOLOGY

By JAMES MARTINEAU, LL.D.

MODERN MATERIALISM: ITS ATTITUDE TOWARDS THEOLOGY.

At the beginning of October, 1874, it was my duty, as Principal of a Theological College, to open a new session with an address, which was afterwards published under the title "Religion as affected by Modern Materialism." It raises the question whether the free and scientific methods of study insisted on in the college involved results at variance with its theological design. It states accordingly three assumptions hitherto implied in that design: "That the universe which includes us and folds us round is the life-dwelling of an Eternal Mind; that the world of our abode is the scene of a Moral Government incipient but not yet complete;

and that the upper zones of human affection, above the clouds of self and passion, take us into the sphere of a Divine Communion." With regard to these assumptions the thesis is maintained that they are beyond the contradiction, because not within the logical range, of the natural sciences. In support of this thesis the mischiefs are shown, both to science and to theology, of confusing their boundaries, and treating the discovery of law as the negation of God; and the separating line is drawn, that in their intellectual dealings with phenomena, science investigates the "how" and theology the "whence." Tempted on by two of its indispensable conceptions, *matter* and *force*, science, overstepping this boundary, has of late affected to know not only the order but the origin of things; in the one case starting them from *atoms* as their source, in the other from mechanical *energy*. I try to show that neither datum will work out its result except by the aid of logical illusions. You will get out of your atoms by "evolution," exactly so much and no more as you have put into them by hypothesis. And, with regard to force, it is contended that observation and induction do not carry us to it at all, but stop with *movements;* that the so-called kinds of force are only classes of phenomena, with the constant belief of causality behind; that of causality we have no cognition but as Will, from which the idea of "physical force" is simply cut down by artificial abstraction to the needs of phenomenal investigation and grouping; and that, in conceiving of the single power hid in every group, we must revert to the intuitive type because the only authorized, and to the highest, because alone covering the highest phenomena. The attempt, under shelter of the unity of energy behind all its masks, to make the lowest phase, besides playing its own part, stand for the whole, is described as a logical sleight of hand by which a heedless reasoner may impose upon himself and others.

After this defensive argument to show that the religious positions are not displaced by natural science, they are traced to their real seat in human nature, and treated as postulates involved in the very existence and life of the reason and conscience. In support of their natural claim to our entire trust, it is contended that, for their ethical power, they are absolutely dependent on their objective truth; and further, that our nature in respect of its higher affections, compassion, self-forgetfulness, moral obligation, is constructed in harmony with a world Divinely ruled, and in utter conflict with the Pessimist's picture of nature.

The address thus epitomized has brought upon me the honor and the danger of a critique by Professor Tyndall,[*] marked by all his literary skill, and rendered persuasive by happy sarcasm and brilliant description. One fault at least he brings home to me with irresistible conviction. He blames my mode of writing as deficient in precision and

---

[*] Fragments of Science: "Materialism" and its Opponents; and, previously, *Fortnightly Review*, November 1, 1875.

lucidity. And I cannot deny the justice of the censure when I observe that my main line of argument has left no trace upon his memory, that its estimate of scientific doctrines is misconstrued, that my feeling towards the order of nature is exhibited in reverse, that I am cross-questioned about an hypothesis of which I never dreamt, and am answered by a charming " alternative " exposition of ascending natural processes which I follow with assent till it changes its voice from physics to metaphysics, and from its premisses of positive phenomena proclaims a negative ontological conclusion. That at every turn I should have put so acute a reader upon a totally false scent rebukes me more severely than any of his direct and pertinent criticisms; for, smartly as these may hit me, they fall chiefly on incidental and parenthetical remarks which might have been absent, or on mere literary form which might have been different, without affecting the purport of my address. Whether the force of these minor thrusts is really disabling, or is only a by-play telling mainly on the fancy of the observer, a brief scrutiny will determine.

(1.) In saying that the college which I represent leaves open to all new lights of knowledge "the special studies which deal with our sources of religious faith," I expanded this phrase by the words, " whether in the scrutiny of nature or in the interpretation of sacred books." This innocent parenthesis, which simply summarizes the growing-grounds of all actual theology, produces in my critic an effect out of all proportion to its significance. Twice he challenges me to show how any "religious faith" can be drawn from " nature," which I regard, he says, as " base and cruel." It suffices to say that " scrutiny of nature " does not exclude " *human* nature," wherein the springs of religion are afterwards traced to their intuitive seats ; and that, in what are called my " tirades against nature," as " base and cruel," I am describing, not my own view of the order of the world, but one which I repudiate as utterly sickly and perverse. Then again, I am asked how, after giving up the Old Testament cosmogony, I can any longer speak of "sacred books," without informing my readers where to find them. I have occasionally met with scientific men whose ideas about the Bible, if going further than the Creation, came to an end at the Flood, and who thought it only loyal to Laplace and Lyell thenceforth to shelve "Moses and the prophets:" but a judgment so *borné* I should not expect from Professor Tyndall. Can a literature then have nothing "sacred," unless it be infallible! Has the religion of the present no roots in the soil of the past, so that nothing is gained for our spiritual culture by exploring its history and reproducing its poetry, and ascending to the tributary waters of its life? The real modern discovery, far from saying there is no sacred literature, because none oracular, assures us that there are several; and, notwithstanding a deepened because purified attachment to our own "Origines" in the Jewish and Christian Scriptures, persuades us to look with an open reverence into all writings that have embodied and sustained the greater pieties of the world. But to my censor it appears a thing incredible that I should find a sanctity in anything human; or deem it possible to approach religion in its truth by intercepting its errors as it percolates through history, and letting it flow clearer and clearer, till it brings a purifying baptism to the conscience of our time.

(2.) In order to give distinctness to that "religion" in relation to which I proposed to treat of "Modern Materialism," I specified "three assumptions" involved in it, of which the first and chief is the existence of the "Living God." I am reproached with making no attempt to verify them, but permitting them to "remain assumptions" "to the end." Be it so, though the statement is not quite exact: still in every reasoned discourse assumptions have their proper place, as well as proofs; and the right selection of propositions to stand in the one position or the other depends on the speaker's thesis and the hearer's needs. My *thesis* was, that natural science did not displace these assumptions, because they lay beyond its range; and the *proof* is complete if it is shown that the logical limit of inductive knowledge stops short of their realm, and is illegitimately overstepped by every physical maxim which contradicts them. To turn aside from this line of argument in order to "verify" the primary matter of the whole discussion would have been to set out for Exeter and arrive at York. My *hearers* consisted of the teachers, supporters, and alumni of a *Theological* College; and to treat them as a body of atheists, and offer proofs of the being of a God, would have been as impertinent as for Professor Tyndall to open the sessions of a *Geological* society with a demonstration of the existence of the earth.

(3.) A few reluctant words must suffice in answer to the charge of "scorning the emotions." I say "*reluctant* words;" for to this side of our nature it is given to speak without being much spoken of; to live and be, rather than be seen and known; and when dragged from its retreat it is so hurt as to change its face and become something else. Here, however, little more is needed than to repeat the words which are pronounced to be so rash and even "petulant"—" I trust that when '*emotion*, *proves empty*, we shall stamp it out and get rid of it." Do I then "scorn" the "emotion" of any mind stirred by natural vicissitudes or moving realities—the cry of Andromache, ^{d}*Ἕκτορ, ἐγὼ δύστηνος*, at the first sight of her hero's dishonored corpse; the covered face and silent sobs of Phædon, when Socrates had drained the cup; the tears of Peter at the cock-crowing; or any of the fervent forms of mental life—the mysticism of Eckhart, the intellectual enthusiasm of Bruno, the patriotic passion of Vane? Not so; for none of these are "empty," but carry a meaning adequate to their intensity. It is for "emotion" with a vacuum within, and floating *in vacuo* without, charged with no thought and directed to no object, that I avow distrust; and if there be an "over-shadowing awe" from the mere sense of a blank consciousness and an enveloping darkness, I can see in it no more than the negative condition of a religion yet to come. In human psychology, feeling, when it transcends sensation, is not without idea, but is a type of idea; and to suppose "an inward hue and temperature," apart from any "object of thought," is to feign the impossible. Color must lie upon form; and heat must spring from a focus, and declare itself upon a surface. If by "referring religion to the region of emotion" is meant withdrawing it from the region of truth, and letting it pass into an undulation in no medium and with no direction, I must decline the surrender.

In thus refusing support from "empty emotion," I am said to "kick away the only *philosophic foundation* on which it is possible to build religion." Professor Tyndall is certainly not exacting from his builders about the solidity of his "foundation;" and it can be only a very light and airy architecture, not to say an imaginary one, that can spring from such base; and perhaps it does not matter that it should be unable to face the winds. Nor is the inconsistency involved in this statement less surprising than its levity. Religion, it appears, has a "philosophical foundation." But "philosophy" investigates the ultimate ground of cognition and the organic unity of what the several sciences assume. And a "philosophical foundation" is a legitimated first principle for some one of these; it is a cognitive beginning—a *datum* of ulterior *quæsita*—and nothing but a science can have it. Religion then must be an organism of thought. Yet it is precisely in denial of this that my censor invents his new "foundation." Here, he tells us, we know nothing, we can think nothing; the intellectual life is dumb and blank; we do but blindly feel. How can a structure without truth repose on philosophy in its foundation?

But do I not myself carry religious questions, in the last appeal, to the inward consciousness of man, whether intellectual for the interpretation of causality, or moral for the interpretation of duty? Undoubtedly; and Professor Tyndall thinks it "highly instructive" that I "should have lived so long, thought so much, and, failed to recognize the entirely subjective character of this creed." If I may omit the word "entirely" (which implies a gratuitous exclusion of "objective truth"), I not only recognize it, but everywhere insist upon it. The fundamental religious conceptions have no deeper validity than belongs to the very frame of our faculties and the postulates of our thinking. But as this equally holds of the fundamental scientific conceptions, as matter and force have also to retire to consciousness for their witnesses, nay, as objectivity itself is but an interpretation by the subject of its own experience, is it not "highly instructive" that a critic so compassionate of my "subjective" position should be unaware of the ideality of his own? Or, has he, perhaps, found some "objective knowledge" which has not to fall back upon a "subjective" guarantee?

If, as I suspect, Professor Tyndall uses the word "subjective not in its strict sense, for what belongs to the *human subject at large*, but to denote what is special to the feeling of *this or that individual*, the question will then be whether I mistake an exceptional personal experience for a universal form of thought. This question is not settled by saying that many able men find in themselves no such inner experience. The eye for correct psychological reading is not secured by great intellect or noble character, but, like the organ of any other art, must be trained to quickness and delicacy of insight; and, while false or over-culture exposes it to the danger of seeing what is not there, a failure of culture may prevent its seeing what there is. Right interrogation and careful comparison alone can sift out the essential from the accidental. Doubtless many a principle once advanced as self-evident and universal survives only in the grotesque museum of philosophers' fancies. But, on the other hand, whatever laws of thought are now admitted as universal were at first propounded, and often long resisted, as the expressions of individual reflection.

(4.) On one point more a personal *éclaircissement* is needed as a condition of any profitable argument. I am said to be "imperfectly informed regarding the position I assail." If I am sensitive to this remark, it is not that I cannot bear to be reminded of my ignorance, the sense of which is a shadow that never quits my life, but that, as no man has a right to attack doctrines which he has not taken the pains to understand, the statement carries in it a moral imputation, and calls on me either to clear it away or to confess a wrong. What then is the "position" which, under the name of "materialism," I intended to assail, and ought, perhaps, to have fixed by exact definition? Professor Tyndall supposes it to be *his* position, regarding which undoubtedly I am very imperfectly informed; for the indications of it, though clear enough for assent or criticism when taken one by one, appear to me so shifting and indeterminate in their combination, as to afford no means of testing it. Except in the two or three passages where it is quoted, the Belfast Address was no more in my view than the writings to which it referred and others belonging to the literature of the subject; and did not supply the form of doctrine to which my argument was addressed. The only question, therefore, is whether that form of doctrine really exists. If it can be shown that I have misconceived the materialists' position, and fastened upon them any thesis which is without eminent representative in their school, I must accept my rebuke. But if no part of my sketch is unsupported by adequate authority, it will remain true, though it should conflict with sentences in the "Fragments of Science."

Probably the chief instance of "imperfect information" is this — that I suppose the materialist doctrine to be offered as an *explanation* of the order of things; for my censor contrasts with this "travesty" of the scheme his own statement, that the materialists' "molecular groupings and movements in reality explain nothing," and that "the utmost he can affirm is the association of two classes of phenomena, of whose real bond of union he is in absolute ignorance. But surely, if this is all that he can affirm, he gives his materialism nothing to do, and is as well off without it as with it: in order simply to see that two series of phenomena run parallel, and correspond term for term, he needs no more than methodized observation, possible and identical on every theory or no theory about the substratum of the phenomena. If the human mind could be content with this spectacle of unexplained concomitance, the very impulse would be wanting from which materialism has sprung. Its fundamental proposition, common, as Lange remarks, to all its forms, ancient and modern,—"that the universe consists of atoms and empty space"*—is an *hypothesis* devised for the

---

* Geschichte des Materialismus, 2tes Buch, p. 181.

express purpose of establishing a "bond of union" between lines of succession previously detached—*i.e.*, of giving the mind a bridge of passage other than that of "association" from the one to the other—*i.e.*, of *explaining* the second by the first. An hypothesis commends itself to us when (*inter alia*) it offers a higher conception from which, as an assumption, we can deduce *both* sets of previously separate facts; and so far as it fails to do this, it is self-condemned. There may be other defects in hypotheses; but if their *data* do not logically lead to the *quæsita*, they break their primary promise; and to see whether they are water-tight throughout, or are leaky at the joints, is an efficient test of their pretensions. A materialist who knows what he is about would not disown the words which I put into his mouth,—"Matter is all I want; give me its atoms alone, and I will explain the universe,"—but would assuredly be offended were he told, and that by a "candid friend," that his doctrine "explains nothing."

As it is impossible to come to close quarters with a see-saw doctrine, which now touches solid ground and now escapes it, I naturally addressed myself to thorough-going materialists, without presuming to commit Professor Tyndall to their consistency. That there have been and are such persons—persons who have undertaken, by defining the essence of matter and fixing it in atoms, " to explain the enigmatical by the clear, the intricate by the simple, the unknown by the known " *— he cannot deny, after having himself introduced us to the thesis of Democritus,† the

---

* Lange, Geschichte des Materialismus, 1tes Buch, pp. 8, 9.

† In connection with this name there is an historical error in the Belfast Address which I should hardly notice were it not likely to be perpetuated by the just reputation of the author, and did it not apparently fall back for support upon Lange. This writer, noticing that Democritus makes no attempt to explain the appearances of adaptation out of the blind power of natural necessity, adds, " Whether this gap lay in his system itself, or only in the tradition of it, we do not know; but we do know that the source of even this last principle of all materialism—rudely shaped, it is true, yet with perfect precision of idea—is to be

reasonings of Lucretius, and the method of Gassendi.* The "atomists," says Lange, "attributed to matter only the simplest of the various properties of things—those, namely,

---

found in the philosophic thought of the Hellenic race. What Darwin, with the support of vast stores of positive knowledge, has effected for the present time, Empedocles offered to the thinkers of antiquity—the simple and penetrating thought that if adaptations preponderate in the world, it is because it lies in their very nature to maintain themselves; while that which fails of adaptation has perished long ago." (I. pp. 22, 23.) Misled by the order of this passage, which gives the missing thought *after* naming the "*gap*" which it might have filled, Dr. Tyndall has described Empedocles as intentionally making good a defect in Democritus—"*Noticing this gap* in the doctrine of Democritus, he (Empedocles) struck in with the penetrative thought," &c. This is an inversion of the chronology. Empedocles preceded Democritus by at least a generation, being born about B.C. 490, and dying B.C. 430; whilst Democritus, whom we find at Thurii shortly after the foundation of the colony in B.C. 443, died at a very advanced age, B.C. 357.—*Diog. Laert.* viii. 52, 56, ix. 41. Comp. Arist. Met. A. 4, p. 985, b. 4.

* Starting from the fundamental assumption, "Principio ergo Universum ex corpore et inani constat, neque enim tertia natura concipi mente præterea potest."—*Phil. Epicur. Syntagma*, Op. T. iii. 11.

which are indispensable for the presentation of a something in space and time; and their aim was to evolve from these alone the whole assemblage of phenomena." "They it was," he adds, "who gave the first perfectly clear notion of what we are to understand by matter as the basis of all phenomena. With the positing of this notion materialism stood complete, as the first perfectly clear and consequent theory of all phenomena."* If there is any difference between this statement of the problem and my "travesty" of it, I cannot discern it.

The indistinctness of which I ventured to complain in Dr. Tyndall's account of his "primordial" datum I do not find removed by my pleasant journey with him to the Caribbean Sea and the Alpine snows, or his graceful pictures of Cingalese ferns, and of nascent infant life. The whole exposition appears to be dominated by the tacit maxim, "No matter without force, no force without

---

* Geschichte des Materialismus, i. pp. 8, 9.

matter "*—a maxim which may be true in fact, but does not dispense with the necessity of investigating the relation between two fundamental ideas which are not identical or interchangeable. In the natural sciences no harm is done by running them both together, or resorting in varying proportions to the one and to the other. Experimental research and mathematical deduction may go on undisturbed, by mere use of them as provisional conceptions, and without even suspecting that they carry in them any ulterior problem. But it is not by thus picking them up *in mediis rebus*, and taking them as they happen to come, that we can reach any philosophical view of the world, or estimate the theories which strive to interpret its unity and meaning. In spite of the cheap wit expended in derision of metaphysics, and the brave preference avowed for *terra firma*, you can escape them only by not knowing where you are. In their embrace you live and move and have your being; and, however fast

---

* Büchner: Kraft und Stoff, p. 2 (Aufl. 4).

your foot may cling to the earth, none the less do you swim with it through the infinite space which even in its emptiness, is yet the condition of all solidity.

At the first glance, nothing looks more hopeful to the enthusiast for simplification than the reduction of "matter" to "force." Two or three easy equations will carry him through the problem. Matter is known to us only by its "properties," and, relatively to us, is tantamount to them. Its properties, again, are only its ways of affecting ourselves, either directly or through operations on other portions of matter. That is, it is represented to us wholly by the *effects* which it has *power* to produce, and resolves itself into an aggregate of *forces*. Make its essence what you will,—extension with Descartes; or palpableness with Fechner,—it is still as acting on the eye or the touch or the muscles that this essence reaches our apprehension; it is the cause of sensations to us, and anything that should cause such sensations would be identical with it. Is it not plain, therefore.

that matter is simply power locally lodged? and that when pursued to its smallest conceivable elements, it merges into dynamic points, unextended centres of attraction and repulsion? Such a course of thought has again and again led to theories of dynamic idealism, like Boscovich's, Ampère's and Cauchy's, in which the dimensions of the atoms whence the molecular action proceeds not simply are small relatively to the distances which separate them, but absolutely vanish. Such theories, by isolating the elements needed for calculation, offer advantages for mathematical physics. But there will always be found an irresolvable residue which declines to melt away into force. When you have construed the atom's solidity into repulsion, and reduced its extension to nothing, here remains its *position*, and this "whereabouts" of a power is other than the power itself; and secures to it a *Da*-seyn or objective existence in space. Nor is the conception of motion adequately provided for in these schemes of abstraction. As geometrical points themselves cannot be moved, the phenomenon becomes a translation of a cluster of attractions and repulsions to new centres. But attraction with nothing to be attracted; repulsion with nothing to be repelled, motion with nothing to be moved, are presentable in language only, not in thought. The running of one eddy round another or into another is intelligible so long as there is a *medium*, be it of ether, however rare; but *in vacuo*, not so. A material *nidus* is indispensable as the seat of every motory change. The reason of this lies in the very structure of the human understanding, which supplies us with the category of Attribute or Property only in combination with that of Substance or Thing as its abiding base. The relation between the attribute which speaks to you phenomenally, and the substance which is given intellectually, is indissoluble: and analyze the phenomena as you may, so as to turn them from one type of predicate to another, you cannot cut them off from their persistent and unyielding seat, so as to have left on your hands a set of predicates without any subject. Thus the idea of "matter" vindicates itself against every attempt to get rid of it by transformation.

The simplification has also been attempted by the inverse method of dispensing with "force," and making "matter" do all the work. In physics, it is said, we know what we perceive or generalize from perception: "we observe what our senses, armed with the aids furnished by science, enable us to observe—nothing more." * *Movements*, however, are all that we perceive, and if at first this fact escapes us when we hear and see, it is because our organs are not fine enough to read the undulations which deliver to them tones and tints. Submit their sensibility to adequate magnifying power, and all that is observable would resolve itself into local changes—molecular or molar. It is the same in the celestial mechanics as in the scene of daily experience. We say that the moon goes through its lunations, and upheaves the tidal

---

* "Materialism and its Opponents," *Fortnightly Review*, p. 595.

wave on the earth spinning beneath it, by the constant force of gravitation. But the real facts noticed are simply the presence now here, now there, of two visible and solid globes, and of some piled-up water upon one of them and a certain rule according to which these changes recur. Were these the only phenomena within our ken, this rule would be all that we mean by the "force" of which we speak. But as there are countless others which we have found to follow the same rule, we cannot speak of it without tacit reference to these, so that the word covers indefinitely more than the facts immediately in view. Still, it takes in nothing in any part of its field but movements and their law. And nothing moves but matter. The natural sciences would thus resolve themselves into a register of co-existent and sequent positions of bodies expressed in formulas as comprehensive as the state of analysis allowed; and in this form, as Compte and Mill justly insist, they would fulfil all the conditions of phenomenal knowledge, and secure that power of *prevision* which is the crown and reward of scientific labor.

This reduction of everything to matter, motion, and law would be unimpeachable, were our intelligence somewhat differently constructed. Matter — as these expositors set out by observing — speaks to our perceptive senses alone; and we should still know it, had we no more than these, and the ability to retain their vestiges and set them in order. Let us only see how things like and unlike lie and move in place and time, and the history of matter is all before us. For this purpose we need not go beyond the relations of objectivity, succession, and resemblance among the forms or data of the understanding. But over and above these we are subject to another determinate condition of thought — the principle of causality — in virtue of which there can be no cognition of *phenomenon*, except as relative to *power* that issues it, any more than there can be a cognition of a *here*, without a *there*, or a *before* without an *after*. This intellectual law leaves us unsatisfied with merely reading the *order* of occurrence among the changes we perceive; it obliges us to refer movement to a motor, to look beyond the matter stirred to a force that stirs it, be the force *without*, as in the expansive energy which propels a loaded shell, or *within* as in that which ultimately bursts it. In any case, you have here a clear dynamic addition to that scheme of regimented and marshalled phenomena which results from the lonely conception of matter. Will you rid yourself of the dualism by insisting, while you concede the power, that it is only a *property* of the matter?

" See," says Lange, " whether here you are not in danger of a logical circle. A 'thing' is known to us through its properties, a subject, is determined by its predicates. But the 'thing' is in fact only the resting-point demanded by our thought. We know nothing but the properties and their concurrence in an unknown object, the assumption of which is a figment of our mind (*Gemüth*), *a necessary one it seems, rendered imperative by our organization.*"*

Another answer may be given thus;—" You may make anything a predicate of matter

---

* Geschichte des Materialismus, ii. p. 214.

which you can *observe* in it *i. e.*, all its *movements;* but not what you *cannot observe,* therefore not the *power* which issues the movements, for this is not seen in the phenomenon; it is supplied by a necessity of thought, not as an element in it, but as a condition of it."

Inasmuch then as both "matter" and "force" are intellectual data (*noümena*), involved respectively in the principle of Objectivity and in that of Causality, neither can be substituted for the other. For ages each has been trying to end the divided sway; but the rival, though often driven from the front, has always found at last an impregnable retreat, whence its rights return to recognition when the usurping rage is past. The present tendency in natural science is so strongly in favor of force as the better known term that, according to Lange, "the untrue element in materialism, viz., the erecting of matter into the principle of all that exists, is completely, and it would seem definitely, set aside."*

From these two roots have arisen two forms

---

* Geschichte des Materialismus, ii. p. 215.

of naturalism, capable no doubt of a balanced co-existence in the same mind, but often unharmonized, and expressing themselves in doctrines doubtfully related to each other. The *material* theory works out the conception of *Atoms*. The *dynamic* relies on that of the *Conservation of energy*. As a means of intellectually organizing ascertained facts, and holding them together in a tissue of conceivable relations, these conceptions possess a high value, and are indispensable to the reaching of any generalizations yet higher. In the one, the multiple proportions of chemistry and the laws of elastic diffusion find an adequate vehicle of expression and computation. In the other, a common measure is set up for variations of heat and mechanical work and chemical decomposition and electrical intensity, bringing several special provinces into a federal affinity. Dr. Tyndall misconstrues me when he imputes to me any disparagement of these conceptions in their *scientific* use, for formulating, linking, and anticipating phenonema. It is not till they break these bounds, and mistaking their own logical character, set up *philosophical* pretensions as adequate data for the deductive construction of a universe without mind, that I venture to resist their absolutism, and set them back within their constitutional rights. It is no wonder, perhaps, that many an enthusiast in the study of nature, excited by the race of rapid discovery, should lose count of his direction as he sweeps along, and, mounted upon these hobbies, should fancy that he can ride off into the region of ontology, and finding nothing, because never really there, should mistake his own failure for its blank. But the calmer critics of human thought know how to distinguish between the physical and the metaphysical use of these conceptions.

"There is scarcely a more *naïve* expression of the materialism of the day," says Lange, "than escapes from Büchner, when he calls the atoms of modern times 'discoveries of natural science,' while those of the ancients are said to have been 'arbitrary speculative representations.' In point of fact, the atomic doctrine to-day is still what it was in the time of Democritus. It has still not lost its metaphysical character;

and already in ancient times it served also as a scientific hypothesis for explanation of natural processes."*

And respecting the law of Conservation of energy, Lange observes that, taken in its " strictest and most consequent meaning it is anything but proved: it is only an '*Ideal of the Reason*,' perhaps however indispensable as a goal for all empirical research." † It is from no want of deference for science proper that I pass again under review the competency of these two doctrines to work out *ab initio*, a blind cosmogony.

The *material* hypothesis, as I read it, and as alone I propose to comment on it, maintains that, with ultimate inorganic atoms to begin with, the present universe could be constructed. Before it can be tested, its *datum* (inorganic atoms) must be pressed into more determinate form by an explanation of the word "atoms." "Things which cannot be cut" might be all alike; or they might be variously different *inter se :* and be-

---

* Geschichte des Materialismus, ii. 181.
† Ibid. p. 213.

fore we start, we must know on which of these two assumptions we are to proceed. The former is the only admissible one, so long as you credit the materialist with any logical exactness. When he asks for *no more than matter* for his purpose, he must surely be understood to require nothing but the *essentials of matter*, the characters which enter into its definition; and to pledge himself to deduce out of these all the accessory characters which appear here and not there, and which discriminate the several provinces of nature. The idea of *atoms* is indeed simply the idea of "matter" *in minimis*, arising only from an arrest, by a supposed physical limit, of a geometrical divisibility possible without end; and the attributes which suffice to earn the one name give the meaning of the other. When in mathematical optics the investigator undertakes, from the conditions afforded by an undulatory elastic medium, to deduce the phenomena of refraction and polarization, he is not permitted to enlarge the data as he proceeds, and surreptitiously import into his other chemical or other characters unnamed at first. Just as little can one who proposes to show the way from simple atoms to the finished world be allowed to swell the definition of those atoms at his convenience, and take on fresh attributes which change them from matter ἁπλῶς, and make them now *this* sort of matter, now *that*. Whatever he thus adds to this assumption is filched from his *quæsita*, to the relief of his problem and the vitiation of its proof : and if the whole fulness of the *quæsita*, is so withdrawn, and turned back to be condensed into *datum*, all deduction is given up, and the thesis is simply taken for granted.

In precisely this plight—unless there is some reasoning between the lines which I am too dull to see—Professor Tyndall leaves his case. He ridicules me for defining the assumed atoms as " homogeneous extended solids," on the ground that a phrase thus restricted to the " requisites of body" gives only " a metaphysical body." * Everything which

---

* It becomes still more metaphysical in the hands

you define is, in the same sense, a "metaphysical" (more properly, a "logical" subject. The object of the definition is to specify the attributes which alone are to be considered in giving the name, and in reasoning from it. The atomist who is not content with my account of his premisses should oblige me with a better, instead of stopping short with the discovery that a definition of a class is not a full description of its individuals. When, however, I look about for my critic's correcter version of "matter" or its atoms, it is long before I learn more than that "we must radically change our notions" of it—an injunction upon which, without further help, it is difficult to act. At length, however, on the concluding page of the critique, the missing

---

of an eminent teacher of physical science. "L'impénétrabilité," says Pouillet, "c'est la matière. On n'a pas raison de dire que la matière a deux propriétés essentielles, *l'étendue* et *l'impénétrabilité*; ce ne sont pas des propriétés, c'est une définition." And again, "L'impénétrabilité inséparable est ce qu'on appelle un *atome*."—*Eléments de Physique expérimentale*, tom. i. p. 4.

definition turns up. "Matter I define as *that mysterious thing by which all this has been accomplished,*" *i.e.*, the whole series of phenomena, from the evaporation of water to self-conscious life of man. Need I say that such a proposition is no definition, and dispenses with all proof; being simply *an oracle* tautologically declaring the very position in dispute, that matter carries in it "the promise and potency of all terrestrial life?" The whole of the picturesque group of descriptive illustration which lead up to this innocent dictum are only an expansion of the same *petitio principii*: they simply say, over and over again, the force immanent in matter *is* matter—they are identical; or if not so as hitherto understood, we will have a new definition to make them so. This is not a process of reasoning, but an act of will —a decretal enveloped in a scientific nimbus. Nothing can be less relevant than to show (and nothing else is attempted) that the forces of heat, of attraction, of life, of consciousness, are attached to material media and organisms, which they move and weave and animate: this is questioned by no one. In the sense of being *immanent* in matter, and manifesting themselves by its movements, they are *material* forces; but *not* in the sense of being derivable from the essential properties or matter, *quâ* matter. And this is the only sense on which philosophies divide, and reasoning is possible.

If the essence of the materialist hypothesis be to start with matter on its lowest terms, and work it thence up into its highest, I did it no wrong in taking " homogeneous extended solids" as its *specified datum*, and its *only* one; so that it constituted a system of "monism." Dr. Tyndall asks me "where and by whom" any such datum is "specified." In the CONTEMPORARY REVIEW, June, 1872, Mr. Herbert Spencer contends that " the properties of the different elements" (*i. e.*, chemical elements, hydrogen, carbon, &c.) " result from differences of arrangement, arising by the compounding and recompounding of *ultimate homogeneous units*." Here, *totidem verbis*, is the monism which I am charged with "putting into the scheme." As my critic is evidently anxious to disclaim the monistic datum, I conclude that he owns the necessity of *heterogeneous elements* to begin with, and feels with me the insecurity of Mr. Spencer's deduction of chemical phenomena from mechanical. Though I have the misfortune, in the use of this same argument—that you cannot pass from the homogeneous to the heterogeneous—to incur the disapproval of two great authorities, it somewhat relieves the blow to find Mr. Spencer at one with the premiss, and Dr. Tyndall ratifying the conclusion.

Before I quit this point I ought perhaps to explain, in deference to Mr. Spencer, why I venture to repeat an argument which he has answered with care and skill. In common with all logical atomists, he appeals to the case of *isomeric* bodies, and especially to the *allotropic* varieties of carbon and phosphorus, to prove that, without any change of elements in kind or proportion, and even without any composition at all, substances present themselves with marked differences of physical and chemical property. There are several distinct compounds formed out of the same relative weights of carbon and hydrogen. And the simple carbon itself appears as charcoal, as black-lead, and as diamond; and phosphorus again, in the yellow, semi-transparent, inflammable form, and as an opaque, dark-red substance, combustible only at a much higher temperature. In the absence of any variation in the material, these differences in the product are attributed to a different grouping of the atoms; and, whatever their form, it is easy, within certain limits, to vary in imagination the adjustments of their homologous sides, so as to build molecules of several types, and ultimately aggregates of contrasted qualities.

I admit that, on the assumption of homogeneity, we may provide a series of unlike arrangements to count off against a corresponding number of qualitative peculiarities, though it is doubtful whether the conceivable permutations can be pushed up through the throng of cases presented by organic chemistry. But the morphological differences, if adequately obtained, contribute no explanation of the observed variations of attribute. What is there in the arrangement $a\ b\ c$ to occasion "activity" in phosphorus, while the arrangement $b\ a\ c$ produces "inertness?" Where the products differ only in geometrical properties, and consequently in optical, the explanation may be admissible, the form and the laying of the bricks determining the outline and the density of the structure. But the deduction cannot be extended from the physical to the chemical properties, so as to displace the rule that to these heterogeneity is essential. To treat the cases of allotropy as destructive of a rule so broadly based, and fly off to a conjectural substitute, is surely a rash logic. In these cases we certainly know of no difference of composition. But neither do we know of any difference of arrangement. The first, if we could suppose it latently there, would be a *vera causa* of the unexplained phenomena; the second, though its presence were ascertained, would still rank only as a *possible* cause of them. If, therefore, an inquirer chose to say, "From this difference of property I suspect a difference of composition," what answer could we give him from Mr. Spencer's point of view? Could we say, "We finally know carbon to be simple?" On the contrary, we are warned that "there are no recognized elementary substances, if the expression means substances known to be elementary. What chemists for convenience call elementary substances are merely substances which they have thus far failed to decompose." If we are to stand ready to see sixty-two out of the sixty-three "elements" fall analytically to pieces before our eyes, how can we feel so confident of the simplicity of phosphorus or carbon, as to make it answerable for a hypothetical reconstruction of chemical laws?

Even in the last resort, if we succeed in getting all our atoms alike, we do not rid ourselves of an unexplained heterogeneity; it is simply transferred from their nature as units to their rules of combination. Whether the qualitative difference between hydrogen and each of the other elements is conditional upon a distinction of kind in the atoms, or on definite varieties in their mode of numerical or geometrical union, these conditions are not provided for by the mere existence of homogeneous atoms; and nothing that you can do with these atoms, within the limits of their definition, will get the required heterogeneity out of them. Make them up into molecules by what grouping or architecture you will; still the difference between hydrogen and iron is not that between one and three, or any other number; or between shaped solids built off in one direction and similar ones built off in another, which may turn out like a right and a left glove. If hydrogen were the sole "primordial," and were transmutable, by select shuffling of its atoms, into every one of its present sixty-two associates, both the tendency to those special combinations, and the effects of them, would be as little deducible from the homogeneous datum as, on the received view, are the chemical phenomena from mechanical conditions. I still think, therefore, that if you assume atoms at all, you may as well take the whole sixty-three sorts in a lot. And this startling multiplication of the original monistic assumption I understand Professor Tyndall to admit as indispensable.

Next, in the striking words of Du Bois-Reymond, I had pleaded the impossibility of bridging the chasm between chemistry and Consciousness. The sensations of warmth, of sound, of color, are facts *sui generis*, quite other than the undulations of any medium, the molecular movements of any structure; known on different evidence, compared by different marks, needing a different language, affections of a different subject; and defying prediction and interpretation, on the part of a stranger to them, out of any formulas of physical equilibrium and motion, or of chemical affinity and composition. They, with all the higher mental conditions, belong to a world beyond the bounds of the natural sciences—a world into which they can *never* find their way, its phenomena being intrinsically inappreciable by their instruments of research. Here, then, in this establishment of two spheres of cognition, separated by an impassable gulf, we surely have a breach in the continuity of our knowledge: on the one side, all the phenomena of matter and motion; on the other, those of living consciousness and thought. Step by step the "Naturforscher" may press his advance, through even the contiguous organic provinces; but at this line his movement is arrested; he stands in presence of that which his methods cannot touch—an intellectual necessity stops him, and that for ever, at the boundary which he has reached. With this doctrine I invited my readers to compare the statement of Professor Tyndall, that, relying on "the continuity of nature," he "cannot stop abruptly where microscopes cease to be of use," but "by an intellectual necessity crosses the boundary, and "discerns in matter the promise and potency of *all* terrestrial life," including, therefore, *conscious* life. *This* statement appeared to me inconsistent with Du Bois-Reymond's "limit to natural science," and still appears so. What is my critic's reply? He cites *another* statement of his, which is quite consistent with the doctrine of the eminent Berlin Professor and anticipates it; a procedure by which he answers himself, not me—and, instead of removing the contradiction, takes it home. If, as the earlier passage says, "the chasm between the two classes of phenomena" (physical processes and facts of consciousness) "remains intellectually impassable," the "intellectual necessity of crossing the boundary" is not easy to understand. In order to "discern in matter the *promise*" of conscious life, you must be able, by scrutiny of its mere physical movements, to forecast, in a world as yet insentient, the future phenomena of feeling and thought. Yet this is precisely the transition which is pronounced "unthinkable;" "we do not possess the intellectual organ, nor apparently any rudiment of the organ, which would enable us to pass, by a process of reasoning, from the one to the other." If between these statements "nothing but harmony reigns," then indeed I am justly charged with being " inaccurate."

How then does the case stand with the atomic hypothesis, as a starting-point of scientific deduction ? In Dr. Tyndall's latest exposition we have it admitted—(1), that the monistic doctrine of homogeneous units will not work, and that the assumption must be enlarged to include heterogeneous chemical atoms; (2), that nothing which we can do with this magnified datum will prevent our being finally stopped at the boundary of consciousness. As these two positions are precisely those which I had taken up against the speculative materialists, it is an infinite relief to discover, when the mask of controversy is removed, the features of a powerful ally. The whole argument sums itself up in Sir William Thomson's remark, "The assumption of atoms can explain no property of body which has not previously been attributed to the atoms themselves."

That the totality of sensible and deducible phenomena is produced by a constant amount of forces in a given quantity of matter is a legitimate principle of modern science, and an adequate key for the interpretation of every proved or probable evolution. And in order to see what is comprised in changes that are intricately woven or fall broadly on the eye, it is often needful to take them to pieces and microscopically scrutinize them. We thus discover more exactly what they are, and how at the moment they are made up; and by doing likewise with the prior and posterior conditions of the same group, we learn to read truly the metamorphoses of the materials before us. But this is all. To suppose that by pulverizing the world into its least particles, and contemplating its components where they are next to nothing, we shall hit upon something ultimate beyond which there is no problem, is the strangest of illusions.

There is no magic in the superlatively little to draw from the universe its last secret. Size is but relative, magnified or dwindled by a glass, variable with the organ of perception: to one being the speck which only the microscope can show us may be a universe; to another, the solar system but a molecule; and in passing from the latter to the former you reach no end of searching or beginning of things. If in imagination you simply recede from the molar to the molecular form of body, you carry with you, by hypothesis, all the properties of the whole into the parts where your regress ceases, and merely substitute a miniature of nature for its life-size, without at all showing whence the features come. If, on the other hand, you drop attributes from the mass in your retreat to the elements, on your return you can never pick them up again: starve your atom down to a hard, geometrically perfect minimum, and you have parted with the possibility of feeding it up to the qualitative plenitude of our actual material forms; for in mere resistance—which is all that is left—you have no source of new properties, only the power of excluding other competitors for its place.

Accordingly, the "atom" of the modern mathematical physics has given up its pretension to stand as an absolute beginning, and serves only as a necessary rest for exhausted analysis, before setting forth on the return journey of deduction. "A simple elementary atom," says Professor Balfour Stewart, " is probably in a state of ceaseless activity and change of form, but it is, nevertheless, always the same."* "The molecule" (here identical with "atom," as the author is speaking of a simple substance, as hydrogen), " though indestructible, is not a hard rigid body," says Professor Clerk Maxwell, " but is capable of internal movements, and when these are excited it emits rays, the wave-length of which is a measure of the time of vibration of the molecule," † "Change of form," and "internal movements" are impossible without

---

* The Conservation of Energy, p. 7.
† A Discourse on Molecules, p. 12.

shifting parts and altered relations; and where, then, is the final simplicity of the atom? It is no longer a pure unit, but a numerical whole. And as part can separate from part, not only in thought but in the phenomenon, how is it an " atom " at all? What is there, beyond an arbitrary dictum, to prevent a part which changes its relation to its fellows from changing its relation to the whole—removing to the outside? Such a body, though serving as an element in chemistry, is mechanically compound, and has a constitution of its own, which raises as many questions as it answers, and wholly unfits it for offering to the human mind a point of ultimate rest. It has accordingly been strictly kept to a penultimate position in the conception of philosophical physicists like Gassendi, Herschel, and Clerk Maxwell, and of masters in the logic of science, like Lotze and Stanley Jevons.

It is a serious question whether, in our time, atomism can any longer fulfil the condition which all the ancient materialism was invented to satisfy. The Ionian cosmogonies sprang from a genuine intellectual impulse; the desire to conquer the bewildering multiplicity of nature, and find some pervading identity which should make a woven texture of the whole; and whether it was moisture, or air, the ether-fire, which was taken as the universal substratum, it was regarded as a *single datum*, on the simplicity of which the mind might disburden itself of an oppressive infinitude. The intention of these schemes was to *unify* all bodies in their material, and in some cases all minds as well, so as not even to allow two originals at the fountainhead, but to evolve the All out of the One. This aim was but an overstraining of the permanent effort of all scientific interpretation of the world. It strives to make things conceivable by simplification, to put what was separate into relation, what was confused into order; to read back the many and the different into the one and the same, and so lessen, as far as possible, the list of unattached and underived *principia*. The charm of science to the imagination and its gain to life may be almost measured by the number of scattered facts which its analysis can bring into a common formula. The very sand-grains and rain-drops seem to lose in multitude, when the morphological agencies are understood which crystallize and mould them. The greatness of Newton's law lies in the countless host of movements which it swept from all visible space into one sentence and one thought. No sooner does Darwin supply a verified conception which construes the endless differences of organic kinds into a continuous process, than the very relief which he gives to the mind serves, with others if not with himself, as an equivalent to so much evidence. The acoustic reduction of sounds, in their immense variety, to the length, the breadth, and the form of a wave, is welcomed as a happy discovery from a similar love of relational unity. To simplify is the essence of all scientific explanation. If it does not gain this end, it fails to explain. Its speculative ideal is still, as of old, to reach some monistic principle whence all may flow; and in this interest it is, especially to get rid of dualism by dissolving any partnership with mind, that materialism continues to recommend its claims. Does it really bring in our day the simplification at which it aims?

Under the eye of modern science Matter, pursued into its last haunts, no longer presents itself as one undivided *stuff*, which can be treated as a continuous substratum absorbent of all number and distinction; but as an infinitude of discrete atoms, each of which might be though all the rest were gone. The conception of them, when pushed to its hypothetical extreme, brings them no nearer to unity than *homogeneity*,—an attribute which itself implies that they are separate and comparable members of a *genus*. And what is the result of comparing them? They "are conformed," we are assured, "to a constant type with a precision which is not to be found in the sensible properties of the bodies which they constitute. In the first place, the mass of each individual," "and all its other properties, are absolutely unalterable. In the second place, the properties of all" "of the same kind are absolutely identical."* Here, therefore, we have an infinite assemblage of phenomena of Resemblance. But further, these atoms, besides the internal vibration of each, are agitated by movements carrying them in all directions, now along free paths and now into collisions.† Here, therefore, we have phenomena of Difference in endless variety. And so it comes to this, that our unitary datum breaks up into a genus of innumerable contents, and its individuals are affected both with ideally perfect correspondences and with numerous contrasts of movements. What intellect can pause and compose itself to rest in this vast and restless crowd of assumptions? Who can restrain the ulterior question,—whence then these myriad types of the same letter,

---

* Discourse on Molecules, by J. Clerk Maxwell, M.A., F.R.S., p. 11.
† Theory of Heat, by J. Clerk Maxwell, M.A., LL.D., F.R.SS. London and Edin. Pp. 310, 311.

imprinted on the earth, the sun, the stars, as if the very mould used here had been lent to Sirius and passed on through the constellations? Everywhere else the likenesses of individual things, especially within the same " species "—of daisy to daisy, of bee to bee, —have awakened wonder and stimulated thought to plant them in some uniting relation to a cause beyond themselves; and not till the common parentage refers them to the same matrix of nature does the questioning about them subside. They quietly settle as derivative where they could never be accepted as original. Some chemists think, as Mr. Herbert Spencer reminds us,* that in the hydrogen atom we have the ultimate simple unit. By means of the spectroscope, samples of it, and of its internal vibrations, may be brought from Sirius and Aldebaran—distances so great that light itself needs twenty-two years to cross the lesser of them—into exact comparison with our terrestrial specimens; and were

---

* Contemporary Review, June, 1872, p. 142.

their places changed, there would be nothing to betray the secret. So long as no *à priori* necessity is shown for their quantity of matter being just what it is, and always the same at incommunicable distances, or for their elasticity and time of pulsation having the same measure through myriads of instances, they remain unlinked and separate starting-points; and if they explain a finite number of resemblances and differences, it is only by assuming an infinite.

But even the approach to simplicity which homogeneity would afford fails us. Notwithstanding the possibility, in the case of certain carbonates, of substituting isomorphous constituents for one another, it cannot be pretended that any evidence as yet breaks down the list of chemical elements: and, should some of them give way before further attempts at analysis, they are more likely—if we may judge of the future from the past—to grow to a hundred than to dwindle to one: to say nothing of the probability, already suggested by the star-spectroscope, that in other regions of space there exist elements unknown to us. At present, in place of a single type of atom, we have to set out with more than sixty, all independent, and each repeating the phenomenon of exact resemblance among its members wherever found. Perhaps you see nothing inconceivable in the self-existence of ever so many perfect facsimiles ready everywhere for the making of the worlds, and may treat it as a thing to be expected that, being there at all, they should be all alike. So much the more certain, then, must be your surprise on finding them *not* all alike, but ranging themselves under sixty heads of difference. If the similars are entitled to the position of ἀρχαί the dissimilars are not: and if neither can prefer the claim, the atomic doctrine, when pushed into an ultimate theory of origination, extravagantly violates the first condition of a philosophical hypothesis.

Nor is its series of assumed data even yet complete. For these sixty kinds of atoms are not at liberty to be neutral to one another, or to run an indeterminate round of experiments in association, within the limits of possible permutation. Each is already provided with its select list of admissible companions; and the terms of its partnership with every one of these are strictly prescribed; so that not one can modify, by the most trivial fraction, the capital it has to bring. Vainly, for instance, does the hydrogen atom, with its low figure and light weight, make overtures to the more considerable oxygen element: the only reply will be, Either none of you or two of you. And so on throughout the list. Among the vast group of facts represented by this sample I am not aware of more than one set—the union of the same combining elements in *multiple* doses for the production of a scale of compounds—of which the atomist hypothesis can be said to render an account. Everything else—the existence of "affinity" at all, its limitation to particular cases so far short of the whole, the original cast of its definite ratios, its preference for unlike elements,—stands unexpained by it, or must be carried into it as a new burden of primordial assumptions. This chasm between the facts of chemistry and its speculations is clearly seen by its best teachers. Kekulé treats the symbolic notation of chemical formulas as a means of simply expressing the *fact* of numerical proportion in the combining weights.

"If to the symbols in these formulas" (he adds) "a different meaning is assigned, if they are regarded, as denoting the atoms of the elements with their weights, as is now most common, the question arises, 'What is the relative size or weight of the atoms?' Since the atoms can be neither measured nor weighed, it is plain that to the hypothetical assumption of determinate atomic weights we have nothing to guide us but speculative reflection." *

The more closely we follow the atomist doctrine to its starting-point, and spread before us the necessary outfit for its journey of deduction, the larger do its demands appear: and when, included in them, we find an unlimited supply of absolutely like objects, all repeating the same internal movements; an

---

* Lehrbuch der organischen Chemie, ap. Lange, Geschichte des Materialismus, ii. p. 191.

arbitrary number of unlike types, in each of which this demand is reproduced; and a definite selection of rules for restricting the play of combination among these elements, we can no longer, in the face of this stock of self-existent originals, allow the pretence of simplicity to be anything but an illusion.

Large as the atomist's assumptions are, they do not go one jot beyond the requirements of his case. He has to deduce an orderly and determinate universe, such as we find around us, and to exclude chaotic system where no equilibrium is established. In order to do this he must pick out the special conditions for producing this particular kosmos and no other, and must provide against the turning up of any out of a host of equally possible worlds. In other words he must, in spite of his contempt for final causes, himself proceed upon a preconceived world-plan, and guide his own intellect as, step by step, he fits it to the universe, by the very process which he declares to be absent from the universe itself. If all atoms were round and smooth he thinks no such stable order of things as we observe could ever arise; so he rejects these forms in favor of others. By a series of such rejections he gathers around him at last the select assortment of conditions which will work out right. The selection is made, however, not on grounds of *à priori* necessity, but with an eye to the required result. Intrinsically the possibilities are all equal, (for instance) of round and smooth atoms, and of other forms; and a problem therefore yet remains behind, short of which human reason will never be content to rest, viz.: How come they to be so limited as to fence off competing possibilities, and secure the actual result? Is it an *eternal* limitation, having its "*ratio sufficiens*" in the uncaused essence of things; or *superinduced* by some power which can import conditions into the unconditioned, and mark out a determinate channel for the "stream of tendency" through the open wilds over which else it spreads and hesitates? It was doubtless in view of this problem, and in the absence of any theoretic means of excluding other atoms than those which we have, that Herschel declared them to have the characteristics of "manufactured articles." This verdict amuses Dr. Tyndall; nothing more. He twice * dismisses it with a supercilious laugh; for which perhaps, as for the atoms it concerns, there may be some suppressed "*ratio sufficiens.*" But the problem thus pleasantly touched is not one of those which *solventur risu;* and, till some better-grounded answer can be given to it, that on which the large and balanced thought of Herschel and the masterly penetration of Clerk Maxwell have alike settled with content, may claim at least a provisional respect.

Having confined myself in this paper to the Atomic Materialism, I reserve for another the consideration of the Dynamic Materialism, and the bearings of both on the

---

* Belfast Address, p. 26. *Fortnightly Review*, November, 1875, p. 598.

primary religious beliefs. To those—doubtless the majority in our time — who have made up their minds that behind the jurisdiction of the natural sciences no rational questions can arise, and from their court no appeal can be made, who will never listen to metaphysics except in disproof of their own possibility, I cannot hope to say any useful word; for the very matters on which I speak lie either on the borders of their sphere, or in quite another. I am profoundly conscious how strong is the set of the *Zeit-geist* against me, and should utterly fail before it, did it not sweep by me as a mere pulsation of the *Ewigkeits-geist* that never sweeps by. Nor is it always, even now, that physics shut up the mind of their most ardent and successful votary within their own province, rich and vast as that province is. "It has been asserted," says Professor Clerk Maxwell, "that metaphysical speculation is a thing of the past, and that physical science has extirpated it. The discussion of the categories of existence, however, does not appear to be in danger of coming to an end in our time; and the exercise of speculation continues as fascinating to every fresh mind as it was in the days of Thales." *

JAMES MARTINEAU.

---

* Experimental Physics, Introductory Lecture, *ad finem.*

MODERN MATERIALISM: ITS ATTITUDE TOWARDS THEOLOGY.

Part II.

It is curious to observe how little able is even exact science to preserve its habitual precision, when pressed backward past its processes to their point of commencement, and brought to bay in the statement of their "first truth." The proposition which supplies the initiative is sure to contain some term of indistinct margin or contents: and usually it will be the term least suspected because most familiar. The student of nature takes as his principle that all phenomena arise from a fixed total of force in a given quantity of matter; and assumes that, in his explanations, he must never resort to any supposed addition or subtraction of either element. In adopting this rule he must know, you would say, what he means by "matter," and what by "force," and that he means two things by the two words. Ask him whence this principle has its authority. If he pronounces it a metaphysical axiom, you may let him go till he can tell you how there can be not simply an *à priori notion* of matter and *notion* of force, but also an *à priori measure* of each, which can guarantee you against increase or diminution of either. As standards of quantity are found only in experience, he will come back with a new answer, fetched from the text-books of science: that his principle is inductively gathered; in one half of its scope—viz., that neither matter nor force is ever destroyed—proved by positive evidence of persistence;—in the other half—viz., that neither is ever created—proved by negative evidence, of non-appearance. If now you beg him to exhibit his proof that matter is indestructible, he will in some shape reproduce the old experiment of weighing the ashes and the smoke, and re-finding in them the fuel's mass: his appeal will be to the balance, his witnesses the equal weights. Weight, however, is force: and thus, to establish the perseverance of *matter*, he resorts to equality of *force*. Again, when invited to make good the corresponding position, of the conservation of force, he will show you how, *e.g.*, the chemical union of carbon and oxygen in the furnace is followed by the undulations of heat, succeeded in their turn by the molecular separation of water into steam, the expansion of which lifts a piston, and institutes mechanical performances: *i.e.*, he traces a series of movements, each replacing its predecessor, and leaving no link in the chain detached. *Movements*, however, are material phenomena: so that to establish the persistence of *force* he steps over to the counsel of *matter*. He makes assertions about each term, as if it were an independent subject: but if his assertion respecting either is challenged, he invokes aid from the other: and he holds, logically, the precarious position of a man rid-ing two horses with a foot on each, hiding his danger by a cloth over both, and saved from a fall by dexterous shifting and exchange.

Nothing can be more unsatisfactory than a scientific proposition, the terms of which stand in this variable relation to each other. The first of them has been sufficiently fixed in discussing the *Atomic* conception. It remains to give distinctness to the second. In order to do so, it will be simplest to follow into their last retreats of meaning the parallel doctrines of the "Indestructibility of Matter" and of the "Conservation of Energy." If our perceptions were so heightened and refined that nothing escaped them by its minuteness or its velocity, what should we see, answering to those doctrines, during a course of perpetual observation?

1. We should see the ultimate atoms; and if we singled out any one of them, and kept it ever in view, we should find it in spite of "change of form," "always the same." "A simple elementary atom," says Professor Balfour Stewart, "is a truly immortal being, and

enjoys the privilege of remaining unaltered and essentially unaffected by the powerful blows that can be dealt against it." * Here, then, we have alighted upon the "Matter" which is "indestructible."

2. These atoms might have been stationary; and we should still have seen them in their "immortality." But they are never at rest. They fly along innumerable paths: they collide and modify their speed and their direction: they unite: they separate. However long we look, there is no pause in this eternal dance: if one figure cease, another claims its place. As in the atoms, so in the molecules which are their first clusters, there is a "state of continual agitation," "vibration, rotation, or any other kind of relative motion;" † "and uninterrupted warfare going on—a constant clashing together of these minute bodies." ‡ In this unceasing *movement* among the "immortal" atoms we alight

---

* The Conservation of Energy, p. 7.

† Theory of Heat, by J. Clark Maxwell, p. 306.

‡ Conservation of Energy, by Dr. Balfour Stewart, p. 7.

upon the phenomenon, or series of phenomena, described by the phrase "Conservation of Energy." So far as the law thus designated claims to be an observed law, gathered by induction from experience, this is its last and whole meaning. We have only to scrutinize its evidence with a little care, in order to see that it simply traces a few transmutations of the perpetual motions attributed to atoms and molecules.

If we chose to shape it thus: "For every cancelled movement or element of movement there arises another, which is equivalent;" everything would be expressed to which the evidence applies. Had we to look out for a proof of such a proposition, we should first consider what it is that makes two movements equivalent: and in the simplest case,—of homogeneous elements,—we should find it in equal numbers with the same velocity; so that the direct demonstration would require that we should count the atoms and estimate their speed. As we cannot count them one by one, we *weigh* them in their masses;—an operation which has the advantage of reckoning at one stroke, along with their relative numbers, also the most important of their velocities. The atoms being all equal, the greater mass expresses the larger number. And weight is only the arrested velocity with which in free space, they move to one another: it is prevented motion, in the shape of pressure. In order to measure it, *i.e.* to express it in terms of space and time, we might withdraw the prevention, and address ourselves to the path that would then be described. But it is more convenient to test it by taking it in reverse, and trying what other prevented motion will avail to stop it and hold it ready to turn back. Thus even statical estimates of equilibrium are but a translation of motion into more compendious terms.

If this is a true account of common weights, it still more evidently applies to the process which gives us the *foot-pound*, or "unit of work:" for this is found by the actual *lifting* of one pound through one vertical foot, *i.e.* by *moving* it through a space in a time. And as in this, which is the standard, so in all the changes which it is employed to measure, the fundamental quantity is simply *movement*, performed, prevented, or reversed.

This fact is easily traced through the proofs usually offered of the Conservation of Energy. The essence of them all is the same:—for each extinguished "unit of work" they find a substituted equivalent movement, molar or molecular. Dr. Joule, for instance, establishes for us a common measure of heat and mechanical work. How does he accomplish this? By applying the descent of a weight to create in moving water friction enough to raise the temperature 1° Fahrenheit; and finding that this result corresponds with a fall of the water through 772 feet. Here, on one side of the equation, we have the movement of the mass through its vertical path; on the other, the molecular movement that constitutes heat; measured by a third movement of an expanded liquid in the thermometer. Where the first is arrested, the second takes its place: and to double one would be to double both.

If heat is made to do chemical work, its undulations are similarly expended in setting up a fresh order of movements; of atomic combination, when burning coal unites with oxygen; of separation, when the fire of a lime-kiln drives its carbonic acid from the chalk. The friction which parts the electricities, the spark which attends their reunion; the crystallization of liquids by loss of temperature, and their vaporization by its increase; the waste of animal tissue by action, and its replacement by food; all reduce themselves to the same ultimate rule,—the exchange of one set of movements or resistances (which are stopped movements) for another, which, wherever calculable, is found to be an equivalent.

To a perfect observer, then, able to follow the changes of external bodies, in themselves, and among one another, to their last haunts, nothing would present itself but consecutions and assortments of phenomena, and arrests of phenomena. And if he had noticed, and could name, what on the subsidence of each group would emerge to replace it, he would be master of the law of Conservation. The sciences would distinguish themselves for him by taking cognizance each of its special set of phenomena; as acoustics tell the story of one kind of undulations, optics of another, thermotics of a third. And the law in question would only carry his glance, as it chased the flight of change, across the lines of this divided work, and show him on the desertion of *this* field, a new stir in *that*.

Though the whole objective world has thus been laid bare before him, and he has read and registered its order through and through, he has not yet, it will be observed, alighted on a single *dynamic* idea: all that he has seen (and nothing has been hid from him) may be stated without resort to any term that goes beyond the relations of co-existence and sequence. The whole vocabulary of causality may absent itself from the language of such an observer. Were it even given to him, it would carry no new meaning, but only tell over again in fresh words the old story of regular time succession. He might, as Comte and Mill and Bain truly contend, command the whole body of science, including its latest law, without ever asking for the origin (other than the phenomenal predecessor) of any change.

By no such ideal interpreter of nature, however, have our actual books of science been written. Never more than now have they abounded in the language which, we have seen, would be superfluous for him. The formula of the new law contains it: for it is the conservation of "Energy," or the correlation of "Forces," which it announces. Are these then some new-comers that we have got to know? or, have we encountered them before under other names, and only found out some new thing about them? "Energy," says Professor Balfour Stewart, is the "power of overcoming obstacles or of doing work."[*]

---
[*] Conservation of Energy, p. 13.

I see a flash of lightning pierce a roof and kill a man and plunge into the earth: the obstacles overcome, the work done, are visible enough; but where is the "power?" what does it add to the phenomenon, over and above these elements? Besides the flash of lightning first, and then the changes in the roof and the man, is there something else to be searched for, and entered, as an object of knowledge, under a separate name? If there be such a thing, by what sense am I to apprehend it? through what aids of art, can I penetrate to it? It is obvious that it has no perceptible presence at all: and that its name stands in the definition and in every inductive equation, as an x, an unknown quantity, which itself has to be found before it can add any new relation to the known. "Force," says Professor Clerk Maxwell, "is whatever changes or tends to change the motion of a body, by altering either its direction or its magnitude."* The shot fired from a gun at a

---

* Theory of Heat, p. 83.

moderate elevation is scarcely out of the muzzle before it quits the straight line for the parabola, and slackens its initial velocity, and soon alights upon the ground. We say the deflection is due to "gravitation." But, if so, this is an invisible part of the fact: no more is observable than the first direction and subsequent curvature of the ball's path, the changing speed, and the final fall, in presence of the earth. The "force" which we superadd in thought is not given in the phenomenon as perceived: and if we know the movements accomplished, prevented, modified, we know everything that is there.

One interpretation, indeed, may be given to these mysterious words which makes them not superfluous, in a methodized account of the order of nature. "Gravitation" perhaps may mean only the *rule of happening* which along with the deflection of the shot, describes also several other cases of movement; and if it enables us to advert to these, while in presence of the immediate fact, it performs a truly scientific function. It is plain, however, that this is not what our Dynamic writers mean. A rule does not " change the motion of a body," does not " overcome obstacles and do work;" nor would any one dream of attaching such predicates to mere similarities of occurrence.

Our instructors then suppose themselves acquainted with more than phenomena, more than the laws of them; and believe that inductive analysis has carried them behind these to " the hiding-place of *power*." They tell us, with much ease and unanimity, what they have found there: so that the story is familiar to every advanced schoolboy, and reproduced in hundreds of examination papers every year. They have found, as sources of the phenomena, a considerable number of " Energies " of nature, which they distinguish from one another in various ways, as " strong " or " weak " as stretching far or keeping near, as demanding the unlike or content with anything, as single or splitting into opposites, as inorganic or organic. In every text-book of science a complete list of these is presented:

and the student, as he learns how to discriminate them, cannot doubt that he is dealing, in each instance, with a separate unit of objective knowledge, which is the inner fountain of a definite set of outward changes. He thus is brought to conceive of nature as having many springs. Its multitudinousness is commanded by a senate of powers.

Further, it is impossible, on looking at the faces of these assembled forces, to assign the same rank to all, or miss the traits of graduated dignity which make them rather a hierarchy than a committee. The delicate precision with which chemical affinity picks its selecting way among the atoms is an advance upon the indiscriminate grasp of gravitation at them all. The architecture of a crystal cannot vie with that of a tree. The sentiency of the mollusk is at an immeasurable distance from the thought which produces the *Méchanique Céleste*. Hence, in the company of powers that conduct the business of nature a certain order of lower and higher establishes itself, which, without settling every point of precedency, at least marks a few steps of ascent, from the mechanical at the bottom to the mental at the top. All equally real, all equally old, they are differenced by the quality of the work they have to do.

On the imagination thus prepared a new discovery is now flung. Keenly watch the face of any one of these forces; its features will change into those of another. You cannot fix its identity in permanence; it migrates from species to species. Now it is mechanical energy; in a minute it will be heat; if a tourmaline is near it will turn up as electricity; and so on, for no part of the cycle is closed against it. You look, in short, upon a row of masks, behind which the "unknown power," slipping away from one to another with magic agility, seems to multiply itself, but is found on closer scrutiny, never to quit its unity. The senate of nature does but administer a monarchy.

And so, the plurality of forces disappears from the ultimate background, and comes to the front as a mere semblance. This brings up a new problem. What stands in the dynamic place thus vacated? How is it related to the disguises it assumes? Do they in any way represent it? or do they only hide it? To this question there are three answers given. (1.) The One Power is indifferently related to all its masks, but is like none of them; they are opaque and let no lineament shine through. (2.) The "phases" are not on an equal footing, but consecutive in their genesis, the *lowest* being the oldest. With *that* the One Power was at first identical, and *that* is what truly represents its essence. (3.) The "phases" are consecutive in their genesis, the *highest* being the oldest. With *that* the One Power is forever identical; all else is its action but not its image. The second of these is the materialist's answer. His preference for it is mainly determined by two reasons. In the first place, since the several forces, A, B, C, D, &c., are all interchangeable, it suffices to allow A (the mechanical), and all the rest are provided for. In the second place, the traces of actual evolution follow this order, conducting us back past the dawn of life, and even the combinations of chemistry, to a period of purely mechanical energy. In estimating these reasons I will step for a moment on to their own ground, and postpone all objection to the theory of " energies " on which they rest.

It is true that, among a number of interchangeables, if the first be given, the others are potentially there. But it is no less true that if the last be given, or any intermediate, there is provision for the rest. The possibility of reciprocal transmutation all round determines no preference of any member as having priority over the rest, and cannot be pleaded as an excuse for selecting the rudest mask of nature as the most faithful likeness of its inner essence. The law of Conservation is impartial, and tells in both directions, exhibiting the elements of the world, here living up into the self-conscious, there dying down into the inorganic, and suggesting, rather than any initial point, circling currents of crossing change.

But further, there is not the slightest ground, in the present transmutations, for treating the lowest phase of force as adequate to the production of the highest. Though mechanical energy, now that it stands in presence of the several chemical elements, may pass into chemical form, it does not follow that it could do so in their absence; for this would be too predicate of homogeneous atoms what we know only of heterogeneous. And the same consideration applies to the phases higher in the scale. *Given*, the existing materials and conditions of life and mind, and the circulation and equivalence of forces may take place as alleged; but that the order could be inverted, and the equivalence avail to provide the conditions, cannot be inferred. Take on the other hand, any higher " phase " as first, and it carries all below it. Chemical force pre-supposes mechanical (as cohesion), and acts at its expense; and vital pre-supposes and modifies the inorganic chemical. In this order of derivation, therefore, the original *datum* would yield what is required by divesting itself of certain conditions admitted to be there, while in the opposite order it would have to take on fresh conditions assumed to be absent at its start. If, in choosing from the phases of force the fittest representative form, we are to be guided by the possibility of deduction, the supreme term must surely be taken as First.

The second plea of the " materialist," viz. that the vista of evolution recedes into the simply mechanical, and is intersected at dimly seen stages by entering lights, first of chemical affinity, then of life, and finally of consciousness, it is the less necessary to qualify as a statement of fact, because it is destitute of logical cogency. Granted that at successive eras these new forces appeared upon the scene, this supplies the " when," but not the " whence " of each. Something more is needful, if you would show that it is the product of its predecessor. Instead of advancing from behind, it may have entered from the side. You cannot prove a pedigree by offering a date. Since these several forces are but secondary phases of a Unitary Power, what obliges us to derive them one from another, instead of letting them all stand in equal and direct relation to their common essence? On this point the first answer to the inquiry after the One Power has a conclusive advantage over the second.

Such, it seems to me, would be the logical position of the materialist's case, on the assumption that separate kinds and transmutation of energy are known* to us, over and above the resulting phenomena, as discoveries of natural science. That assumption, hitherto conceded, I must now withdraw. No "energy" has ever come under human notice, and disclosed its marks, so as to discriminate itself from others, similarly apprehended. This is not simply true thus far as a matter of fact: it is true permanently as a matter of necessity. We might watch for ever the relations of bodies and their parts *inter se*, and though we had eyes that ranged from the microscopic minimum to the analysis of the milky way, we should fetch no force into the field of view: and the whole story of what was laid open to us would be a record of interminable series and eddies of change. What are called the " transmutations of energy " are nothing but transitions from one chapter of that record to another. A certain catena of phenomena runs to an end; the first link of a new one is ready to take its place: a body's fall is stopped; its temperature rises: the thermometer in the kettle ascends to 212° Fahrenheit and stays there; the water turns to steam : this is observed, and no more than this. And the list of metamorphosed energies deceives us, if we take it for anything beyond an enumeration of these junctures between class and class of consecutive movements. Did we bring to the contemplation of nature no faculties but those which constitute our scientific outfit, I see no reason to believe that it would come before us under any other aspect; or that we should ever be tempted to paint its picture or tell its history in dynamic terms.

Are such terms then illusory? Are they

susceptible of no meaning? or of only a false meaning? Far from it. The thought that is in them we cannot indeed fetch out of nature: but we are obliged to carry it into nature. To witness phenomena and let them lie and dispose themselves in the mere order of time, space, and resemblance, is to us impossible. By the very make of our understanding we refer them to a *Power* which issues them: and no sooner is perception startled by their appearance than the intellect completes the act by wonder at their source. This "power" however, being a postulate intuitively applied to phenomena, and not an observed function found in them, does not vary as they vary, but mentally repeats itself as the needed prefix to every order of them: and though it may thus migrate, now into this group, now into that, it is the dwelling alone which changes, and that which is immanent is ever the same. You can vary nothing in the total fact, except the collocations of material conditions; out of which, as each new adjustment emerges, the persistent power elicits a different result. Instead of first detecting many forces in nature and afterwards running them up into identity, the mind imports one into many collocations; never allowing it to take different names, except for a moment, in order to study its action now here, now there. If this be true, if causality be not seen, but thought, if the thought it carries belongs to a rule of the understanding itself, that every phenomenon is the expression of power, two consequences follow: the plurality of forces disappears: and, to find the true interpretation of the One which remains, we must look not without but within; not on the phenomena presented, but on the rational relations into which they are received. Power *is* that which *we mean by it;* nor have we any other way of determining its nature than by resort to our self-knowledge. The problem passes from the jurisdiction of natural science to that of intellectual philosophy. Thither let us follow it.

I have already hinted that if we were mere passive, though thinking, observers of the world around us, we should witness phenomena without asking for a power: the principle of causality would remain latent in the intellect: the occasion would be wanting which permits it to awake. That occasion is furnished by the active side of our nature, by our own spontaneous movement from its inner centre out upon objects near its circumference. Being conscious as originators of the exercise of power, we admit as recipients its exercise upon us: nor is causality conceivable except upon these meeting lines of action and reaction; any more than, in the case of position, a *here* is conceivable without a *there*. Both pairs, the dynamic and the geometrical, are functions of the same fundamental antithesis, of subject and object, which is involved in every cognitive act. Till we disengage ourselves from nature, we do not think though we may feel: and when we disengage ourselves from nature, we are self-conscious subjects and objects of casual operation. The idea of power coming in this dual form, as out from us and on to us, its two sides are reciprocally related: and that which the inner side is to the *object*, the same is the outer side to the *subject*. With the inner side, however, we are intimately familiar: it is the one thing which we immediately know; unless, indeed, it sits so near our centre as rather to regulate our knowing than stand off enough to become itself the known: but in any case we have to mark it by a name, as the inmost nucleus of dynamic thought: and we call it living *Will*. This is our causality; and it is what we mean by causality: in the absence of this, no other source for the idea, in the presence of this, no other meaning for it, can be found. It is true that of the reciprocal propositions, "We push against the wind," "The wind pushes against us," we know the force named in the first with a closeness not belonging to our knowledge of the other. We cannot identify ourselves with the wind as our own *nisus* is identified with us. We go out on an energy: we return home on a thought. But that thought is only the reflex of the energy; it has, and can have, no other type. Our whole idea of *Power* is identical with that of Will, or reduced from it. That which, in virtue of the principle of causality, we recognize as immanent in nature, is homogeneous with the agency of which we are conscious in ourselves. Dynamic conceptions have either this meaning, or no meaning: cancel this, and you cut them at the root, and they wither into words; and your knowledge, cast out into dry places, has to take refuge again with co-existences and successions. Whatever authority attaches to the law of causality at all attaches to it, presumably at least, in its intuitive form,— phenomena are the expression of living energy; and cannot be reduced within narrower limits, unless by express disproof of coincidence between its natural range and its real range. Till that disproof is furnished, the One Power stands as the Universal Will.

I am aware what courtesy it would require in a modern *savant*, whether of the Nescient or of the Omniscient school, to behave civilly to such folly as this must seem to him: nor can I pretend to find his laughter a pleasant sound: for I honor his pursuits, and sorrowfully dispense with his sympathy. It makes amends, however, that even among the most rigorous scientific thinkers, some curious testimony or other from time to time turns up to the correctness of the interpretation just given of the idea of power. Even Gassendi, the modern Epicurus, the eager disciple of Copernicus and Galileo, cannot refrain from resorting to living and conscious action in explanation of physical. To render the earth's attraction intelligible he has two favorite devices. He lays it down that every whole nature has a sort of clinging affection for all its parts, and resists their being torn or kept away from it; so that the earth sends out invisible arms or tentacula to fetch back objects detached from it: and hence the fall of the rain, the hail, the stone from the sling.* And he institutes a double compari-

---

* De motu impresso a Motore translato, xii. Opera, Lugd. 165, tom. iii. p. 491.

son;—first assimilating the earth to a magnet; and then the magnet's force to the fascinating or repulsive influence of objects upon the senses,—the sweetness of the rose, which draws us to it, the noisomeness of a drain, that drives us away.* In this appeal to "sympathy" and "antipathy" we see again, as already in the φιλία of Democritus, how inevitably the imagination, even when most intent on keeping within physical limits, is betrayed into mental analogies. Not a few indeed, of the most clearsighted men of science have been well aware of the real source of our dynamic conceptions; in some cases accepting it as authoritative, in others being ashamed of it as a mere occasion of superstition. Redtenbacher, in his "Principles of Mechanical Physics," refers our knowledge of "the existence of forces to the various effects which they produce, and *especially to the feeling and consciousness of our*

---

* Syntagma Philos. Phys. sect. iii. mem. I. lib. iii. p. ii. Op. 132; and De motu impresso xiii. tom. iii. p. 492.

own forces." * And in conversation with Fechner, Professor E. H. Weber laid stress on the fact that in the will to move the body occurs the only case of immediate consciousness of power operative on matter, and accordingly identified the essence of power with that of will, and from this principle worked out his religious ideas.† That it is not, however, in the mere interest of a religious theory that this doctrine finds its strength, it is evident from its hold on Schopenhauer, who, in virtue of it, would call the inward principle of nature nothing but *will*, though striking out from that name whatever makes its meaning divine. Herschel's judgment, often criticized but never shaken, was deliberately pronounced :—

"That it is our own immediate consciousness of *effort* when we exert force to put matter in motion, or

---

* Das Dynamidensystem, Grundzüge einer mechanischen Physik, p. 12, ap. Lange; Gesch. d. Materialismus, ii. p. 205.

† Fechner, Ueber die physikalische und philosophische Atomenlehre; 2te Aufl., p. 132 (note).

to oppose and neutralize force, which gives us this internal conviction of *power* and *causation* so far as it refers to the material world, and compels us to believe that whenever we see material objects put in motion from a state of rest, or deflected from their rectilinear paths and changed in their velocities if already in motion, it is in consequence of such an *effort somehow* exerted, though not accompanied with *our* consciousness."*

With the tone of this memorable statement it is interesting to compare the feeling of one who, owning the same psychological fact, treats it as an infirmity, instead of accepting it as a guide.

"Power, regarded as the cause of motion, is nothing," says Du Bois-Reymond, "but a more recondite product of the *irresistible tendency to personify* which is impressed upon us;—a rhetorical artifice, as it were, of our brain, snatching at a figurative turn of thought, because destitute of any conception clear enough for literal expression. In the notions of Power and Matter we find recurring the same dualism which presents itself in the ideas of God and the world, of soul and body; the same want which once impelled men to people bush and fountain, rock, air and sea with

---

* Treatise on Astronomy, 1833. Ch. vii. § 370.

creatures of their imagination. What do we gain by saying it is reciprocal Attraction whereby two particles of matter approach each other? Not the shadow of any insight into the nature of the process. But, strangely enough, our inherent quest of causes is in a manner laid to rest by the involuntary image tracing itself before our inner eye, of a hand which gently draws the inert matter to it, or of invisible tentacles, with which the particles clasp together, try to seize each other, and at last twine together into a knot." *

This outburst of exasperation against all dynamic conception,—for to that length it really goes,—is justified if the human mind has nothing to do but to become an accomplished Naturforscher. It is quite true that "insight into the nature of the process" is gained only by a closer reading of its steps in their series and in their analogies, and is in no way aided by passing behind the movements they comprise. What then? Shall we be angry at our propensity to look behind them, and tear it from our nature under vows

---

* Untersuchungen über thierische Electricität. I. Bd. Berlin, 1848. Vorrede, S. xi. ap. Lange's Gesch. d. Mat. ii. 204.

to reach a stainless intellect? We shall but emasculate the mind we wish to purify: for what is the nerve of its vigor but the very Wonder which is for ever seeking an unattainable rest? If we incessantly press into nature, it is in hope of finding what is beyond nature: and all that we have learned of the finite world indirectly comes from our affinity with the embracing Infinite. It would be strange if the Causal appetency which no disappointment wears out, should be at once our greatest strength and our most fatal illusion. It is admitted to be "irresistible:" it is admitted to carry the belief of personality: but these features, which induced Herschel to yield to it and trust in it, are reasons with Du Bois-Reymond for resisting and despising it. I need hardly say that, when he calls its language "figurative" and its conception a "personification," he oracularly assumes the very point at issue. To "personify" is to invest with personality that which has it not: and to tell any one with Herschel's belief that he does this is only to contradict him. So again, if you know that there are two things of different type, living power and dead power, and then transfer to the second the marks of the first, your language is "figurative:" but if to you the types are identical, the second coinciding with the first, you speak with literal exactitude; and to charge you with rhetoric is only to beg the question in dispute. Probably the writer was the less conscious of any dogmatism here, from his thoughts already running upon the stock example of belief in the Pagan gods of "rock and air and sea,"—fairly enough adducible as a departed superstition. But the dying out of Polytheism is misconceived if it be regarded as an expulsion of every Conscious Presence from venerated haunts, and the substitution of a dead for a living world. It was a fusion, not an extinction, of Will; as the little cantons of nature, once under independent guardians, melted into ever wider provinces, and clans of men clustered into confederated nations, the detected harmony of the kosmos and the felt unity of humanity carried with them the enthronement of a single Divine Mind in place of the vanished local gods. It is not that other and other powers have been discovered, but that fewer and fewer have been needed, till the plurality is lost in One Supreme. And as, with the widening scope of the natural order, the many wills lapsed into one, so, among monotheists, did the many motives of that One, once so freely attributed, more and more merge themselves in the recognition of an all-comprehending scheme, whose thoughts were not acts but laws, and whose purpose flowed into the inlets of individual life from an ocean of universal relations. By this surrender of providence *in exiguis* we drop the quest of design in events taken one by one, and learn to speak of the power which produces them, and to divide it into lots, not according to their supposed aims, but according to their visible kinds: and thus it is that by suspending the idea of an end in view the full-bodied notion of Will is attenuated to that of Force.

How imperfectly, even then, the life is driven out of it, may be seen from Du Bois-Reymond's expostulation with it. And the suspended idea only flits away to settle upon a higher point. Instead of having discovered that *purpose is not there*, we have simply learned that purpose takes in more; and the little pulses of separate volition are lost in the mighty movements of Eternal Thought.

In the remarkable passage which I have quoted, and in the argument of which it forms a part, Du Bois-Reymond puts Matter and Force on the same footing, and discharges the former as well as the latter from the realm of reality, by reducing it also to an empty abstraction. He is led to this position by that just logical appreciation which gives to his writings, as to those of Helmholtz, a high philosophical rank, in addition to their value as models of scientific exposition and research. The equipoise, true enough, is perfect, in respect to validity, between the ideas of Matter and of Power: and the only question is, whether both are to be dismissed as illusions, or both retained as intuitive data of thought, the conditions of all construed experience. To reject them both is practically impossible, though logically necessary if you part with either. To retain them both is simply to accept the fundamental relation of object and subject under its two constitutive functions, instead of treating our only modes of knowing as snares of ignorance. The existence of a Universal Will and the existence of Matter stand upon exactly the same basis, of certainty if you trust, of uncertainty if you distrust, the *principia* of your own reason. For my part, I cannot hesitate. Shall I be deterred by the reproach of "anthropomorphism?" If I am to see a ruling Power in the world, it is folly to prefer a man-like to a brute-like power, a seeing to a blind? The similitude to man means no more and goes no further than the supremacy of intellectual insight and moral ends over every inferior alternative: and how it can be contemptible and childish to derive everything from the highest known order of power rather than the lowest, and to converse with Nature as embodied Thought, instead of taking it as a dynamic engine, it is difficult to understand. Is it absurd to suppose mind transcending the human? or, if we do so, to make our Reason the analogical base for intellect of wider sweep? How is it possible to look along any line of light traced by past research, and, estimating the contents which it reveals, and leaves still unrevealed, to remember that along all radii to which we may turn a similar infinitude presents itself to any faculty that seeks it, and yet to conceive that this mass of truth to be known has only our weak intelligence to know it? And if two natures know the same thing, how can they be other than like? Nay, Du Bois-Reymond himself takes up the magnificent fancy of Laplace, of a "mind cognizant of all forces operating in nature at a given moment, and all mutual relations among the beings composing it. Such a mind, if in other respects capacious enough to subject these data to analysis, would comprise in the same formula the movements of the greatest masses in the universe, and of the lightest atom. Nothing would be uncertain to him; and to his glance future and past would alike be present. The human understanding presents, in the perfection to which it has brought astronomy, a feeble image of such a mind."* Here is reproduced the very thought which, in his ignorance of differential equations, Plato expressed by saying that God was the supreme Geometer; simply taking to the summit-level the analogy which Laplace leaves floating at some indefinite height above the human. Is the conception, then, vitiated because it is "anthropomorphic?" Let Du Bois-Reymond answer, "Wir gleichen diesem Geist, denn wir begreifen ihn."† If to have the idea of a diviner nature is to resemble him, and if resemblance must be reciprocal, what can be more futile than the reproach that men attribute to God what is highest in humanity.

---

* Ueber die Grenzen des Naturerkennens, p. 6.
† Ibid. p. 10.

It may be doubted, indeed, whether the analogy might not be pressed further, without overstraining its truth. If the collective energies of the universe are identified with Divine Will, and the system is thus animate with an eternal consciousness as its moulding life, the conception we frame of its history will conform itself to our experience of intellectual volition. Its course is ever from the indeterminate to the determinate; and as the passage is made by rational preference among possibilities, thought has its intensity at the outset, and action in the sequel. It is in origination, in disposing of new conditions, in setting up order by differentiation, that the mind exercises its highest function. When the product has been obtained, and a definite method of procedure established, the strain upon us is relaxed, habit relieves the constant demand for creation, and at length the rules of a practised art almost execute themselves. As the intensely voluntary thus works itself off into the automatic, thought, liberated from this reclaimed and settled province, breaks into new regions, and ascends to ever higher problems: its supreme life being beyond the conquered and legislated realm, while a lower consciousness, if any at all, suffices for the maintenance of its ordered mechanism. Yet all the while it is one and the same mind that, under different modes of activity, thinks the fresh thoughts and carries on the old usages. Does anything forbid us to conceive similarly of the kosmical development;—that it started from the freedom of indefinite possibilities and the ubiquity of universal consciousness; that, as intellectual exclusions narrowed the field, and traced the definite lines of admitted movement, the tension of purpose, less needed on these, left them as the habits of the universe, and operated rather for higher and ever higher ends not yet provided for; that the more mechanical, therefore, a natural law may be, the further is it from its source; and that the inorganic and unconscious portion of the world, instead of being the potentiality of the organic and conscious, is rather its residual precipitate, formed as the Indwelling Mind of all concentrates an intenser aim on the upper margin of the ordered whole, and especially on the inner life of natures that can resemble him? I am aware that this speculation inverts the order of the received kosmogonies. But, in advancing it, I only follow in the track of a veteran physiologist and philosopher, whose command of all the materials for judgment is beyond question,— the author of "Psychophysik." Fechner insists that protoplasm and zoophyte structure, instead of being the inchoate matter of organization, is the cast-off residuum of all previous differentiation, stopping short of the separation of animal from plant and of sex from sex, and no more capable of further development than is inorganic matter, without powers beyond its own, of producing organization.* And, far from admitting that the primordial periods had few organisms, which time increased in number, he contends that

---

* Einige Ideen zur Schöpfungs-und Entwickelungsgeschichte der Organismen, p. 73.

the earth was formerly more rich in organisms than now, and that the inorganic realm has grown at the expense of the organic." *

The resolution of all power into Will is met by the thorough-going objection, that Mind is not energy at all, and can never stir a particle of matter. "Were it possible," says Lange, "for a single cerebral atom to be moved by 'thought' so much as the millionth of a millimetre out of the path due to it by the laws mechanics, the whole 'formula of the universe' (*i.e.*, as imagined by Laplace) would become inapplicable and senseless." †
"Suppose," he adds, "two worlds, both occupied by men and their doings, with the same course of history, with the same modes of expression by gesture, the same sounds of voice, for him who could *hear* them—*i.e.*, not simply have their vibrations conveyed through the auditory nerve to the brain, but be self-conscious of them. The two worlds are therefore to be absolutely alike,

---

* Einige Ideen zur Schöpfungs-und Entwickelungs geschichte der Organismen, p. 73.

† Geschichte des Materialismus, ii. p. 155.

with only this difference: that in the one the whole mechanism runs down like that of an automaton, without anything being felt or thought, whilst the other is just *our* world; then would the formula for these two worlds be completely the same. To the eye of exact research they would be indistinguishable." *

So much the worse, are we not tempted to say, for " exact research?" If, with all its keenness and precision it misses half the universe, and identifies diametrical opposites, it will be perhaps, a calamity rather for it than for us, that its " formula " should prove less applicable than had been supposed. The extension to man, in an exaggerated form of Descartes' doctrine of animal automatism marks, perhaps, the lowest point which the falling barometer of philosophy has reached. By him it was propounded for the express purpose of finishing off the mechanical modes of action, even when strained to their maximum, short of the human characteristics; and of opening in these a second and sharply

---

* Ibid. ii. p. 156.

contrasted world, containing another hemisphere of phenomena, with their own lines of causality and relations of affinity. Though by his absolute separation of matter and mind he cut the problem of the world in two, he at least embraced the whole of it, and attempted to solve it by a double formula. But his modern interpreters do not see why one half of his theory should not be stretched to do the work of the whole: they have only to ignore his unmechanical part of the world and leave it out in the cold, and in place of his contrast they will get an identity. For his maxims,—Movement is the cause of movement, Thought of thought, but neither of the other,—they substitute the rule that Movement is the cause of both, but Thought of neither: so that there is no longer any counterpart to the mechanism of nature, or any work done beyond it; and whatever puffs of thought and screeches of feeling there may be, it is only that the engine is blowing off its steam: nothing comes of it, and it may be treated as waste. This theory is founded on the analysis of reflex action in the nervous apparatus, in which the sensory conductor having delivered its stimulus in the ganglion, the motory takes up the sequence and contracts the muscles requisite for action in response. If the brain be kept from interfering the circuit is completed in unconsciousness; and its series, though determining the subject to all sorts of clever and congruous movements, is composed of molecular changes unattended by feeling or design. When the scene is transferred to the brain or connected with it, the story, we are assured, is still the same, only with the added phenomenon of consciousness. In the one case, the subject acts: in the other, he acts and knows it. But this new fact is inoperative, and leads to nothing: were it absent, he would figure away as a molecular automaton all the same, and not a scene or a word would be altered in the five-act comedy of life. Comparing in this view the reflex and the cerebral activities, we might say that the former resembles a clock with *one beat*—viz., movement only; the latter, a clock with *two beats*—viz., movement *plus* consciousness.

By the extent of this increment, the second does more work than the first. What, then, becomes of the difference? Where are we to look for it at the next stage? We are expressly told it has no next stage, and things will go on exactly as if it had not been there. Then a portion of work has perished, and the Conservation of energy is contradicted.

The only escape from this conclusion would be by denying that consciousness produced is " work done." This, however, is to admit that it is not an effect of molecular forces; to exempt it altogether from the range of physical law; and to throw it into an independent world of its own, beyond the jurisdiction of the natural philosopher. Such a position would be an unconditional relapse into the two-armed embrace of Descartes, from which the whole doctrine is a struggle to escape.

It is said that if thought can move a single molecule, the law of causality is at an end.

Why is it not equally at an end if, conversely, molecular movement can wake a single thought? Either way, causality alike steps out of the material series, and crosses over to the other, now last, now first. And it is only on the assumption that it cannot do this, being a monopoly of Physics, that the objection has any sense.

This doctrine, that the most important elements of life,—all that constitute experience, and embody themselves in language, art, religion,—are so much *surplusage*,—that the mental phenomena are collectively a *cul-de-sac*, leading nowhither,—comes with a singular irony from men who by force of intellect, knowledge and character are in many ways changing the conceptions of their time, and whose most signal triumph it will be to convince us that, if they never felt or thought at all, or stirred emotion and idea in us, it would make no difference to our history, and the senseless pantomime of our life would fit into the same niche in the world's "formula." Such paradoxical triumphs are occasionally won by planting the old nightmare of necessity closely on our breast. But not for long: and the first of us that, feeling cold, spreads his hands before the fire, or, struck with grief, wrings them over the lifeless features of a friend, will here break the spell, and restore the faith that to be conscious, to think, to love, is to have power.

But then, it is said, this mental power, even if we concede it, is found only in connection with definite material conditions; in the absence of which, as in the structure of plants, we have no grounds for admitting any conscious life.

" What can you say then to the student of nature if, before he allows a Psychical principle to the universe, he asks to be shown, somewhere within it, embedded in neurine and fed with warm arterial blood under proper pressure, a convolution of ganglionic globules and nerve-tubes proportioned in size to the faculties of such a Mind?"*

"What can we say?" I say, first of all, that

---

* Du Bois-Reymond, Ueber die Grenzen des Naturerkennens, p. 37.

this demand for a Divine brain and nerves and arteries comes strangely from those who reproach the Theist with " anthropomorphism." In order to believe in God, they must be assured that the plates in " Quain's Anatomy" truly represent him. If it be a disgrace to religion to take the human as measure of the Divine, what place in the scale of honor can we assign to this stipulation? Next, I ask my questioner, whether he suspends belief in his friends' mental powers till he has made sure of the contents of their crania? and whether in the case of ages beyond reach, there are no other adequate vestiges of intellectual and moral life in which he places a ready trust? *Immediate* knowledge of mind other than his own he can never have : its existence in other cases is gathered from the signs of its activity, whether in personal lineaments or in products stamped with thought: and to stop this process of inference with the discovery of *human* beings is altogether arbitrary, till it is shown that the grounds for extending it

are inadequate. Further, I would submit
that, in dealing with the problem of the Universal
Mind, this demand for organic centralization
is strangely inappropriate. It is
when mental power has to be localized,
bounded, lent out to individual natures and
assigned to a scene of definite relations, that
a focus must be found for it and a molecular
structure with determinate periphery be built
for its lodgment. And were Du Bois-Reymond
himself ever to alight on the portentous
cerebrum which he imagines, I greatly
doubt whether he would fulfil his promise and
turn theist at the sight: that he had found
the Cause of causes would be the last inference
it would occur to him to draw;
rather would he look round for some monstrous
creature, some kosmic megatherium,
born to float and pasture on the fields of
space. The great " energies " which we
recognize as modes of the Universal Power
are not central but ubiquitous: gravitation
reports itself whenever there is a particle of
matter; heat and light spread with the

ether whose undulations they are; and electricity, at one moment gathered into poles, at another sweeps in the aurora over half the heavens. But if still my questioner cannot dispense with some visible structure as the organ of the Ever-living Mind, I will ask him, in his conception of the brain to take into account these words of Cauchy's:—

"Ampère has shown . . . that the molecules of different bodies may be regarded as composed each of several atoms, the dimensions of which are infinitely small relatively to their separating distances. If then we could see the constituent molecules of the different bodies brought under our notice, they would present to our view sorts of constellations; and in passing from the infinitely great to the infinitely small we should find, in the ultimate particles of matter, as in the immensity of the heavens, central points of action distributed in presence of each other."*

If then the invisible molecular structure and movement do but repeat in little those of the heavens, what hinders us from invert-

---

* Cited from Moigno's Cosmos, tom. ii. p. 374, by Fechner: Atomenlehre, xxvi. p. 232.

ing the analogy, and saying that the ordered heavens repeat the rhythm of the cerebral particles? You need an embodied mind? Lift up your eyes, and look upon the arch of night as the brow of the Eternal, its constellations as the molecules of the universal consciousness, its space as their possibility of change, and the ethereal waves as the afferents and efferents of Omniscient Thought. Even in the human nerves, the solid lines are but conductors, and the granules but media of movement; and science is ever on the search for some subtler essence that is thus sheathed and transmitted. In the kosmos, then, think of that essence as unsheathed and omnipresent, with light for its messenger and space for its scope of perception, and your material requisition is not wholly a dream.

Quite in the sense of Du Bois-Reymond's objection was the saying of Laplace, that in scanning the whole heaven with the telescope he found no God; which again has its parallel in Lawrence's remark that the scalpel, in opening the brain, came upon no soul.* Both are unquestionably true, and it is precisely the truth of the second which vitiates the intended inference from the first. Had the scalpel alighted on some perceptible ψυχή, we might have required of the telescope to do the same; and, on its bringing in a dumb report, have concluded there was only mechanism there. But, in spite of the knife's failure, we positively know that conscious thought and will were present, yet no more visible, yesterday: and so, that the telescope misses all but the bodies of the universe and their light avails nothing to prove the absence of a Living Mind through all. If you take the wrong instruments, such quæsita may well evade you. The test-tube will not detect an insincerity, or the microscope analyze a grief. The organism

---

* Both these dicta I quote from memory, without at the moment being able to verify the citations. An equivalent passage to the latter occurs in the "Lectures on Physiology, Zoology, and the Natural History of Man," p. 8, 1819.

of nature, like that of the brain, lies open in its external features, to the scrutiny of science: but, on the inner side, the life of both is reserved for other modes of apprehension, of which the base is self-consciousness and the crown is religion.

The contempt or sorrow with which the claim of *design* is struck out from the interpretation of the world results in like manner from a false start in construing the dynamic idea. We are supposed to have made acquaintance, in the laboratory, the botanic garden, the aquarium, and among the stars, with a set of blind forces to which a happy hit and a stupid blunder are indifferent and possible, alike; and then by way of supplement to these, to introduce into the thus prepared scene the action of intellectual purpose. The former is treated as the sphere of determinate causality; the latter of teleological government. It is plain that, under these conditions, nothing is left to the second agency except the residue unexplained by the first; nor does anything suit its character except the fitness which (*inter alia*) are not impossible to the other also. Unless therefore it invades and interrupts the series otherwise inevitable, it is liable to be deposed and "mediatized" by advancing knowledge; its troop of anomalies filing off by degrees into the drilled army of necessity; and the adaptations it had claimed being traced to the forces which cannot think. With these logical preconceptions, it is no wonder that the naturalist directs a professional enmity against the doctrine of design, and meets it as the opponent he is for ever beating back: and as he is certainly not only in his right, but at his duty, in pushing to the utmost his researches into the physical history of the forms and phenomena he studies, it is a venial impatience with which he resents attempts to stop him by "supernatural phantoms" across his path. If he can display the mechanism by which the heliotrope turns to the sun, or the chemistry by which in a few hours the turbot assumes the color of the ground over which it swims, or tell the whole story which, beginning with a jelly-point tingling in the sunshine, ends with the completed human eye, let his work have all sympathy and honor. But if he imagines that he is displacing Thought from nature by discovering causality, he is the subject of the very same illusion which would cry him down and arrest his course. The cases do but present the two sides of one superstition.

The dispute between acting Force and intending Mind is as unmeaning as the quarrel of a man with his own image. The two are identical,—expressions, now in all dimensions, now in some, of the same nature. Causal power other than Will being an unknown quantity, nay, absolutely out of the sphere of thought, teleology and causality are incorporated in one; and mechanical necessity, instead of being the negation of purpose, is its persistence,—the declining, no doubt, of this or that possible diversion to minor ends, but in subservience to the stability of a more comprehensive order. The inexorability of nature is but the faithfulness of God, the maintenance of those unswerving habits in the universe, without which it could train no mind and school no character: and that it is hard and unbending to us does not prevent its being fluid to Him. To affirm *purpose* therefore in the adjustments of the world is not to set up a rival principle outside their producing force, but to plant, or rather to leave, an integrating thought within it. And, conversely, to trace those adjustments to their " physical causes," is not to withdraw them from their ideal origin, but only to detect the method of carrying the inner meaning to its realization. Who will venture to say, what nevertheless is constantly imagined, that to find how a change comes about is to prove that it was never contemplated? If it *were* contemplated it would have to be executed *somehow;* if, the moment you read the machinery provided for this purpose, the purpose itself is quenched from your view, is this the discovery or the loss of a reality?

This treatment of determinate causation as incompatible with conscious aims is the more curious, as proceeding from a school which, as necessarian, is constantly laboring to show the co-existence of the two in human nature. If man is only a sample of the universal determinism, yet forms purposes, contrives for their accomplishment, and executes them, definite causality and prospective thought can work together, and the field which is occupied by the one is not preoccupied against the other.

The frequent pleas, "See, there is no mind here, for all is necessary causation," tacitly concedes that, in order to have mind, there must be exemption from necessity; and can be consistently urged only by one who attributes this exemption to the human will. Is the argument conclusive from his point of view? It would be so, were it possible to prove his premiss, viz., the universality in the kosmos of necessary causation. But this is plainly out of the question, because his amplest science carries the induction, such as it is, only skin-deep into the universe; because he would have to show that the present fixity was not determined by a past exercise of will; because Mind, in proportion as it is orderly and exact in its methods, may assume the semblance of necessity, and be the less suspected that its freedom works by rule. He knows how he himself, though conscious of self-disposal as well as of subjection to nature, presents to the determinist the aspect of a machine; and how can he be secure against a similar illusion in his interpretation of the world? What is to prevent the same combination of free and necessary causality which he finds in himself from existing also beyond? Nay, if there were only mind-excluding force in nature, how could there arise a force-resisting mind in him? He could not carry in himself new causal beginnings, if in the kosmos whence he comes the lines of possibility were definitely closed.

I revert, then, after weighing these objections, to my "unwiderstehlicher Hang zur Personification," and persist in regarding that which the natural philosopher calls *force*, and Professor Tyndall raises to an immanent *life*, as Causal Will, manifesting itself, not in interference with an established order, but in producing it. As it builds and weaves and quickens all matter, and could not otherwise work before us at all, the structures and growths of the material world are its seat, and their phenomena its witnesses: so that the very story,—of saline crystals, and ice-stars, and fernfronds, and human birth,—which Professor Tyndall tells in order to exclude it, is to me a continuous report of its agency and laws. He asks, what else is there here than matter? I answer, the *movement* of matter, with their disposing and "formative *power*," the attracting and repelling energies, which, *dealing with* molecules and cells, *are not* molecules and cells. "Mens agitat molem." Whoever finds this incredible will soon have to make friends with some abstraction which is but a ghastly mimicry of it; for *some* conception over and above that of "pure matter," is indispensable to the accurate representation of the simplest facts. If in the typical "oak-tree" the vitality suddenly ceased, the "matter" of it would at the next moment still be there, as certainly as that of a clock which had run down: it would weigh the same as before, and so stand the admitted test of the indestructibility of matter. Yet *something* is gone which was previously there, and that something has to be described otherwise than in terms of "matter." The droll "hypothesis" which my critic amuses himself with conjecturally attributing to me, "of a vegetable soul," wedded to the tree at a definite date, and quitting it when its term was up, certainly does not help us; and is set up on my behalf, I presume, simply from the facility of knocking it down. But are we any better served by the "alternative" conception of a "formative power," long latent and "potential," *i.e. not* forming anything, but only *going to do so?* I see that the conception contradicts Büchner's dictum, "A power not expressing itself has no existence;" yet am at a loss to know how, during its latency, its presence is ascertained, and to exercise with regard to it "that Vorstellungs-fähigkeit with which, in my efforts to think clearly, I can never dispense." Whilst it lies in wait behind the scenes,—before the time for the deposit of the crystal or the germination of the acorn,—*where* is it? behind what molecules does it hide? through what space is it invisibly present? What shape has it, enabling it to lay its building particles and to agglutinate cells? How does it know the right moment of temperature for stepping on to the stage, and declaring itself without further reserve? In short, all the questions addressed to me respecting the "formative soul" invented for me, I refer back to be answered on behalf of my critic's "potential power." "Potentiality" is an intelligible fact in a being consciously able to act or to refrain. But when the idea is carried into a system of necessitated phenomena, it means nothing in *them*, but something in *us*, as their observers—viz., that we conditionally anticipate a future change, forseeing a distant term of a series which would be certain, provided the nearer ones were not obscure. To plant this subjective suspense out into the field of nature to do objective work there, now alighting visibly upon the earth, and then hidden again in "an ambrosial cloud," is a sort of intellectual illusion which modern logic might have been expected to cast out.

In truth, the nearer I approach the Power which Professor Tyndall pursues through nature with so subtle and brilliant a chase, and the more I try, by combining the predicates which he gives and withholds, to think it out into the clear, the less distinct does this "ideal somewhat" become, not simply to the imagination, but to intellectual apprehension. A power which is not Mind, yet may be "potential" and exist when and where it makes no sign; which is "immanent" in matter, yet *is* matter; which "is manifested in the universe," yet is not "a Cause," therefore has no effects; presents to me, I must confess, not an overshadowing mystery, but an assemblage of contradictions. I have always supposed that "Power" was a relative word, and that the correlative was found in the "work done:" take away the latter by denying the causation, and the term drops into five letters which might as well be arranged in any other order.

Yet elsewhere this negative language is balanced by such large affirmative suggestions that I almost cease to feel the interval between my critic's thought and my own. Of the inorganic, the vegetable, and the animal realms, he says—

"From this point of view all three worlds would constitute a unity, in which I picture life as immanent everywhere. Nor am I anxious to shut out the idea that the life here spoken of may be but a subordinate part and function of a higher life, as the living, moving blood is subordinate to the living man. I resist no such idea, as long as it is not dogmatically imposed. Left for the human mind freely to operate upon, the idea has ethical vitality; but stiffened into a dogma, the inner force disappears, and the outward yoke of a usurping hierarchy takes its place." *

---

* *Fortnightly Review*, November, 1875, p. 596.

Bidding God-speed to this sudden flank-attack upon usurping hierarchies and dogmas, I pursue only the main line of march in the free "idea." Whither does it lead me? It shows me the three provinces which make up our kosmos blended into one organism by an all-pervading life, which conducts all their processes, from the flow of the river to the dynamics of the human brain. This alone brings me to a pause of solemn wonder,—a single power through the whole, and that a living one! But there is more behind. This power, co-extensive though it is with nature, is not all: beyond her level we are to think of a "higher life," to which her laws and history do but give functional expression. May we then really think out this "idea" of a life "higher" than what is supreme in the world, — higher, therefore, than the human? But scale of height above that point we do not possess, except in gradation of intellectual and moral sublimity; and either that Ideal Life must cease to live, or must come before our thought as transcendent Mind and Will, on a scale comprehending as well as permeating the universe. With any guide who brings me hither I sit down with joy and rest. It is the mountain-top, which shows all things in larger relations and through a more lustrous air; and every feature,—the great build of the world close at hand; the thinning of the everlasting snows, as they stoop and melt towards human life; the opening of sweet valleys below the earlier and wilder pines; and the final plains, teeming in their silence with industry and thought, — is better understood than from level points of view, where the scope is narrowed or the calm is lost. But my guide seems less content than I to rest here, and deserts me, not, so far as I can trace him, to reach a brighter point, but rather to descend into the mists. To the "higher life," transcending our highest, he dares not give the predicate "Mind," or apply the pronoun of Personality.* On *what* scale, then, is it "higher?" If not on the intellectual and

---

* *Fortnightly Review*, November, 1875, p. 596.

moral, then there is that in man which rises above it; for the power of attaining truth and goodness is ideally supreme. If Professor Tyndall can reveal to us something which is higher than Mind and Free Causality, by all means let us accept it at his hands and assign it to God. But in order to profess this, and therefore to deprecate as an " anthropomorphism," the ascription of a mind to Him, one would have, I think, to be one's self something *more than man*. Only such a one could cast a look above the level of Reason, to see whether it was overtopped: and so, this fashionable reproach against religion is virtually an arrogating of a superhuman position. As we cannot overfly our own zone, no beat of our wings availing to lift us out of the atmosphere they press, surely, if that " higher life " speaks to us in idea at all, it can only be as Perfect Reason and Righteous Will. Those who find this type of conception not good enough for them,—do they succeed in struggling upwards to a better? Rather, I should fear, does a persistent gravitation gain upon them, till they droop and sink into the alternative faith of blind force which leaves their own rank supreme.

Professor Tyndall sets the belief in " unbroken causal connection" and the " theologic conception " over against each other as " rivals ; " and says that an hour's reasoning will give the first the victory.* The victory is impossible, because the rivalry is unreal. Why should not a Mind of illimitable resources,—such as " the theologic conception " enthrones in the universe,— conduct and maintain " unbroken causal connection ? " Is not such connection congenial with the relations of thought and the harmony of intellectual life? Do not you, the student of nature, yourself admire it ? Is it not the theme of your constant praise ? Do you not speak with contemptuous aversion of alleged deviations from the steadfast tracks of order? and would you not yourself maintain those tracks, if you were at the head of things ? To this attitude you are impelled by a just

---

* *Fortnightly Review,* November, 1875, p. 596.

jealousy for the coherent beauty and worth of science as a whole. If, then, these unswerving lines so dignify the investigating intellect which regressively traces them up, how can it be out of character with the Mind of minds to think them progressively forth?

In the discussion which here reaches its close my object has been simply defensive,— to repel the pretension of speculative materialism to supersede "the theological conception," by tracing the pretension to an imperfect appreciation of the ultimate logic of science. But the idea of Divine Causality which is thus saved, though an essential condition, is not the chief strength of religion; giving perhaps its measure in breadth, but not in depth. Were the physical aspect of the world alone open to us, we should doubtless gain, by reading a divineness between the lines, for beauty a new meaning, for poetry a fuller music, for art a greater elevation; but hardly a better balance of the affections or more fidelity of will. It is not till we cross the chasm which stops the scientific continuity, not till we make a new beginning on the further side, that the "idea of a higher life," emerging now in a far different field, can claim its "ethical value." The *self-conscious* hemisphere of inner experience,—which natural philosophy leaves in the dark,—*this* it is which turns to its Divine Source; and finds, not in any vacant "mystery," but in the living sympathy of a supreme Perfection, " the lifting power of an ideal element in human life." Only by converse with our own minds can we—to use the words of Smith of Cambridge—"steal from them their secrets," and " climb up to the contemplation of the Deity."[*] It is but too natural that this inner side of knowledge, this *melior pars nostri*, should be unheeded by those who look on it as the mere accessory fringe of an automatic life, gracefully hanging from the texture, but without a thread of connection beyond; and that with them the

---

[*] Discourse iii., p. 66. ap. Tulloch's Rational Theology, vol. ii. p. 158.

word "subjective" should be tantamount to "groundless." They confess the "mystery" of this interior experience only to fly from it and refuse its light. Yet here it is that at last light and vision lapse into one, and supply the ἡλιοειδέστατον τῶν ὀργάνων * for the apprehension of the first truths of physical and the last of hyperphysical knowledge. Till we accept the "*faiths*" which our faculties postulate, we can never *know* even the sensible world; and when we accept them, we shall know much more. Short of this firm trust in the bases whereon our nature is appointed to stand,—a trust which, if destroyed by a half-philosophy, must be restored by a whole one,—the grandest "ideas" flung out to play with and turn about in the kaleidoscope of possibilities, or work up as material of poetry and rhetoric, can no more "lift" a human will than the gossamer pluck up the oak on which it swings. Unless your "ideal" reveals the real, it has no power, and its "ethic value" is that of a dissolving

---

* Plato de Rep., 508, A.

image or a passing sigh. You must "*be-lieve*," ere you can "remove mountains:" if you only fancy, they sit as a nightmare on your breast. And if man does nothing well, till he ceases to have his vision, and his vision rather has him and wields him for action or repose; and if then he astonishes you with his triumphs over "nature" and her apparent real, is he the *only* being who thus rides out upon a thought, and makes the elements embody it? Have not these elements already learned their obedience, and grown familiar with the intellectual mandate to which they yield? A man truly possessed, ethically moulded by the pressures of reverence and love, you can never persuade that the beauty, the truth, the goodness which kindles him is but his private altar-lamp: it is an eternal, illimitable light, pervading and consecrating the universe. Unless it be so, it fires him no more: and, instead of utterly surrendering his will to it in trust and sacrifice, he begins to admire it as a little mimic star of his own, —a phosphorescence of matter set up by the chemistry of nature, not to see things by, but to glisten on the darkness of himself. It is vain to expatiate on the need of religion for our nature, and on the elevation of character which it can produce, and in the same breath bid it begone from the home of truth and seek shelter in the tent of romance. If its power is noble, its essence is true. And what that essence comprises has been worked fairly out in the long experiment of Christianity on human nature; which has shown that in its purest and strongest phase, religion is a variety and last sublimity of *personal affection* and living communion with an Infinitely Wise and Good and Holy. The expectation that anything will remain if this be dropped, and that by flinging the same sacred vestments of speech round the form of some empty abstraction you can save the continuity of piety, is an illusion which could never occur except to the outside observer. Look at the sacred poetry and recorded devotion of Christendom: how many lines of it would have any meaning left, if the conditions of conscious relationship and immediate converse between the human and the Divine Mind were withdrawn? And wherever the sense of these conditions has been enfeebled, through superficial "rationalism" or ethical self-confidence, "religious sterility" has followed. To its inner essence, thus tested by positive and negative experience, Religion will remain constant, taking little notice of either scientific forbearance or critical management; and, though left, perhaps, by temporary desertion to nourish its life in comparative silence and retirement, certain to be heard, when it emerges, still speaking in the same simple tones, and breathing the old affections of personal love, and trust, and aspiration.

www.ingramcontent.com/pod-product-compliance
Lightning Source LLC
Chambersburg PA
CBHW031818220426
43662CB00007B/702